GW00470418

A Puppy the Size of a Pony

Grace Dorey

Edited by Claire Makin

ryelands

To Nick, for everything

*To Claire, Martin, Jo, Maggie and Charlie for being such a
wonderful family*

To all dog-lovers, who have a perfect pet. I am envious.

*To those dog-owners, who understand the frustrations
of owning a wilfully defiant dog, who has made
unpredictability into a career path. This is for you.*

Front cover: *photograph by Tom Teegan*
Back cover: *William enjoying the wet sand*

First published in Great Britain in 2011

Copyright © Grace Dorey 2011

All rights reserved. No part of this publication may be reproduced,
stored in a retrieval system, or transmitted in any form or by any
means without the prior permission of the copyright holder.

British Library Cataloguing-in-Publication Data
A CIP record for this title is available from the British Library

ISBN 978 1 906551 28 5

RYELANDS
Halsgrove House,
Ryelands Industrial Estate,
Bagley Road, Wellington, Somerset TA21 9PZ
Tel: 01823 653777   Fax: 01823 216796
email: sales@halsgrove.com

Part of the Halsgrove group of companies
Information on all Halsgrove titles is available at: www.halsgrove.com

Printed and bound in Great Britain by CPI Antony Rowe, Wiltshire

CONTENTS

ACKNOWLEDGEMENTS

My gratitude goes to Glennis Hewitson for breeding my beautiful pedigree Golden Retriever puppy and for kindly letting me have him despite serious reservations. You were right to be concerned.

I am indebted to my talented cousin, Claire Makin, for kindly agreeing to edit a third book.

Most importantly, I would like to thank Nick for chuckling each time I recounted William's triumphs and disasters, but most of all for encouraging me to write a sequel to *Barking Mad in Barnstaple* and *William: Still Barking* to complete the trilogy.

Grace Dorey

Chapter 1

STILL UNPREDICTABLE

William has endeared himself to many, many readers, so I felt I had a duty to continue writing my diary recounting his various and oft-times crazy exploits. For the last two years, this glorious Golden Retriever has captured my heart (and I hope yours) with his stunning good looks and charming disposition. He has also brought me to the brink of total frustration with a medley of misdemeanours as long as an orang-utan's arm, each designed to pit his wits against me and win. I, on the other hand, have not relinquished my Alpha role and have continued to train my dog, in the hope that one day, hopefully one day soon, he will become totally controlled, though I would settle for anything from 'mildly obedient' upwards.

In January 2009, I presented a book-reading of *Barking Mad in Barnstaple*, my first William book, to a band of seasoned dog-lovers in The New Inn at Roborough, Devon. These experts reckoned that Goldies are not keen to settle down until they are ten years old! *"Rats!"*, I thought. *"So there's no hope for a two-year-old pickle with multiple mischievous tendencies."* Then one lady mentioned that she had three dogs from the same parentage; two were obedient and one was monstrously uncontrolled. Had I landed up with the headstrong monster of his litter? Would my recalcitrant adolescent ever obey instructions sufficiently to impress even the most devoted of dog-lovers?

When I was in France last year with my partner, Nick, we saw a mature Golden Retriever walking beside his master along a slim pavement bordering a busy main road. Surprisingly, he was not attached to a lead. At each shop, this loyal dog waited patiently outside for his master to emerge, then they walked together across a zebra crossing and disappeared up the hill (into the sunset). I was filled with a mixture of admiration and envy at this remarkable display. How had they arrived at this point? How many years of training had this super-dog undergone? Would William ever lose his adventurous streak and walk to heel in the same impressive way? I did not know why I bothered to ask these questions; I knew all the answers only too well. William was his own chap and along with other coves of a similar type, he answered to no-one! Not unless it suited him.

If there is a tasty titbit in sight, he will come inside when called, unless he has a better game to play, which usually consists of rushing round the garden with a stolen object in his mouth. Sometimes, the object is alive and kicking and takes the form of a rabbit, mouse or bird, when he is too quick and artful to allow me to save his prey. His method of exterminating these hapless small animals is to roll over them.

One day, I was clearing out a room in the barn, ready for it to be converted into a bedroom for my guests, and I left two cacti outside the door ready to take into my cottage. To my astonishment, out of the corner of my eye, I saw young William rushing down the garden with a cactus in his mouth. Fearful that he may be harmed by the spikes or even suffer as a result of their poisonous secretions, I called: "Come William." No response. I then shouted: "Come William!" before I followed him deep into the garden. I might as well have been bellowing at the stone wall. William emptied the pot, ate all the plant-fibre, and left the prickly part on the concrete drive. End result: a very dead cactus, a thoroughly frustrated owner, and another black mark for my over-excited and decidedly-determined dog.

My cactus-strewn oasis turned into a snowfield overnight; four inches of fluffy flakes fell, the first snow that I had seen in Devon since my arrival ten years ago. My rambling garden looked surreal; like a beautiful, unspoiled scene that would have made the most perfect Christmas card. Before I could reach for the camera to capture this stunning snow scene, William went ballistic. He sprang out of the kitchen, skidded down the steps and proceeded to eat as much of the white stuff as possible. He pushed his nose under the snow in a series of determined spade-like manoeuvres (in the same way as he attacks mud and sand), each designed to carve out a narrow channel while covering his face completely in snow.

This he did with his tail wagging in orgasmic ecstasy, as he rolled, nosed and head-butted the snow until the lawn changed from a virginal white sheet to a very messy battlefield. He barked for me to join him but, disappointingly for him, I stood my ground.

I had stocked up with food the day before (not because I had listened to the forecast, but because I was down to my last knob of cheese and a few shooting potatoes, so I knew I could weather the storm for a week. My daughter, Claire, telephoned from London to say that the city was at a standstill with no public transport running; she was not venturing out, for fear of falling over. My son, Martin, rang to advise me not to attempt to drive down my steep driveway in the ice. Then he announced that he was unable to get to the office, so was taking Maggie and Charlie (my grand-daughters) and Bob (the mongrel) tobogganing. It sounded fun. How William would have loved it, but he was confined to the garden and would have to make his own entertainment. Later, I felt guilty and succumbed, so threw a few bitterly-cold snowballs for him to catch, but as his catching skills were nil, he missed every single one, before scrabbling frantically for a white snowball in the snow. There was not a lot of hope for him!

I had to pop on Wellington boots to go across to my new office in the Barn to collect my emails, mostly from similarly snow-bound friends, with whom I commiserated at length. I cancelled my indoor tennis and also my continence clinic at the Nuffield Hospital, Taunton, the following day. Even Saunton Sands, known for its warmer mini-climate, was covered in snow. This magical surfing beach was shown in all its arctic glory on the national television news.

While I was on the telephone, I noticed some deep footprints coming from the Barn, where a young couple were holidaying. They must have left their car in the lay-by the previous night and been unwilling to attempt my steep icy drive. This young couple had come to Devon to surf and had chosen the worst week of the decade! I heard subsequently from Dave, the Master Carpenter, that unfortunately the young lady had hit her head on the rocks and needed three stitches, so on the third day of their week's holiday, they went home without leaving any messages, save for her bikini pants, which were covering the fire alarm situated over the bed – like a trophy.

The snow thawed out, only to be replaced by a rainy, drizzly, messy Monday; the sort of day when the depressed dream of suicide, leaving me wishing for the pretty white stuff to return. Unashamedly, I spent the day keeping warm and cosy in bed reading *A Home for Rose*, a delightful book by Jon Katz. Jon is a professional writer, who bought a farm in upstate New York so that his three sheepdogs could hone their herding skills (and so that he could write their story). One of them, Devon, whose name was changed mysteriously to Orson (why?) used to terrorise the sheep. His second dog, Homer, whose herding skills were wanting, was terrorised by both Orson and Rose, the new puppy, so Homer was sadly re-homed to become the star of a one-dog family. Rose, however, as a result of Jon's training and about 95% instinct, became a remarkably gifted and cunning shepherd.

I was immensely upset when Jon made the heart-wrenching decision to send Homer away and saddened every time he visited his ex-pet, particularly when this devoted dog looked as if he wanted to follow his ex-master home. Then, I thought of my previous Golden Retriever, Mischa, who, at the age of five, left Glennis, my friend who bred William, and her lively pack of six dogs to live with me. Mischa settled in brilliantly as she enjoyed being the one-and-only (who doesn't?), and although she moved in from the cottage next-door, she never wanted to return. In fact, just the opposite. When she was left with Glennis, while I was away lecturing, she escaped (twice) and each time she was found sitting happily on my kitchen doorstep!

Glennis and I had considered re-homing William when, as a young puppy, he bit my grand-daughter Charlie's sleeve and refused to let go. It was a decision I was unable to make; I adored my young grandchildren and would not have exposed them to the danger of a wilful and ebullient puppy, but by that time I had fallen headlong in love with young Wills. I decided to take Glennis's advice and keep him in his cage when the children visited. When we went for family walks, William was fine with the little ones; he was free, less excited and had his own agenda exploring all the sights, sounds and smells of the countryside.

During one walk, he suddenly stopped and held up his right front paw. With a plaintive look in his eyes, he turned his head up to me and silently expressed: *"Please could you take this painful prickle out of my paw?"* Indeed, there was the largest thorn in Devon spiking menacingly into his pad; I removed it and we continued on our walk. It would have been nice to have had some thanks, but I guess I have never taught him how important it is to show even a glimpse of gratitude. I know he is devoted to me; he follows me around and nuzzles me and he loves all the stroking, patting and cuddling that I give him. I forgave him his poor manners; his undying devotion was more than enough thanks for me.

On Valentine's Day 2009 I had owned William for two years, so I took him for a walk, just the two of us, to celebrate this special event. I thought about how far we had progressed in getting to know each other's personality, habits and foibles. I had learned not to leave anything within reach of his vice-like jaws; he had learned to sit politely before being allowed to eat and to walk demurely on the lead. He adored people. If anyone called, he would bark louder than a pack of hungry wolves, jumping vertically at my kitchen window until I opened the door.

That weekend, Kym and Philip came to stay for a special romantic weekend in my Barn. As I was greeting them, William was busy barking his own special welcome through the kitchen window.

Kym asked: "Is that William?".

"How do you know his name?" I replied curiously.

"I've read his book," she announced.

William was fast becoming a tourist attraction! For my guests, the celebratory weekend, commencing with pink champagne and Belgian chocolates in their love nest, was a cracking success and certainly eclipsed the effort that I had made to mark the two years that Wills and I had been together. By way of a consolation prize, and maybe because she felt that she now knew the star of the book, Kym thoughtfully gave William a pot of bubbles as a going-home present.

After my delightful guests had left, I decided that Wills and I should play together. I blew a myriad of tantalising bubbles, which drifted up, up and away, while Wills looked on with disdain. I blew some more perfect diaphanous spheres, but all he could muster was an arrogant look which conveyed: *"I used to play with these when I was a puppy, but why should I bother to catch something that bursts on impact, is inedible and only makes my nose soapy."*

When he was a young puppy, he went wild with delight, trying to catch each bubble for safe-keeping. He leaped into the air like an ungainly high-jumper, with legs akimbo, tail dancing and mouth poised wide-open in preparation for collecting as many of the spherical delicacies as possible. He enjoyed the time of his life, with a mixture of wonderment, bewilderment and raw excitement. What a difference two years had made. He was starting to settle down.

CHAPTER 2

CRUFTS 2009 AND FLYING DOGS

I decided that I should try to get *Barking Mad in Barnstaple* on sale at Crufts, to make it available to other ardent dog lovers. I emailed Halsgrove Publishing to ask if they could help. They replied that they would contact their distributor, Gardners Books, and ask them to alert their book-sellers. As this was rather in the lap of the gods, I decided to contact some of the book-sellers myself. Only one of them showed any interest. Ring Press Books wanted a staggering 40% commission, which meant that for a small printing run, Halsgrove would be selling at a loss. I declined.

As I still had a box of *Barking Mad* flyers, I asked Glennis if she would kindly place them on the Golden Retriever stand. She readily agreed, so I drove round to her house with the precious flyers. I asked if she would be showing Frankie (William's handsome brother) this year but was told that he was currently moulting and that his coat was too threadbare. I showed her William, who was sitting beautifully in the boot of my car.

"His coat is really thick and furry, I could have shown him, but he hasn't qualified for Crufts," Glennis said.

I looked at my handsome dog and at his luscious coat and delighted in his furriness. "Ahah!" I laughingly replied. " You chose the wrong puppy at birth!"

Glennis subsequently told me that she kindly flew round the show distributing a few flyers to each stand, before showing Reggie (Gatchell's Lone Ranger) in the Golden Retriever Class. Reggie, the product of Champion parents, was William's father and unfortunately not placed. Glennis said she would like to take William to a local show, but would need to groom him by clipping his masculine chest fur and trimming his swishy tail. William declined, as he was, like me, rather attached to his fur.

I met Glennis and her mother, Olive, for morning coffee. Glennis's lovely father, Tom, had recently died, so I gave Olive a few pink roses and a warm hug before extending my heartfelt sympathy.

"How are you coping?" I asked.

" I'm able to go out more now and see more people," she bravely replied, "but I am very lonely at night." I suggested that she might perhaps like to get a dog for company, to which Glennis quickly quipped: "Are you trying to re-home William?". Olive quietly replied: "No thank you, Grace, I have read your book!"

I showed Glennis and Olive the recent conversion to my barn, which elicited gasps of admiration at the high specification of the interior décor in the bedroom and bathroom. I think if we had stayed in the new garden room any longer, they would have been tucked up in bed! Everything in the bedroom is white; the walls, the linen and the en suite, which contrast magnificently with the old oak beams and bespoke oak furniture. A dusky pale turquoise is tastefully introduced by the bedside lamps and the exquisite Laura Ashley silk cushions. I was proud of the room and looked forward to showing my daughter, Claire, who is a renowned interior designer.

William was destined for another kennel holiday, as I particularly wanted to see Bryen and June in Bushey. Bryen was terminally ill with secondaries from prostate cancer and bravely coping with an almost unbearable amount of pain. The plan was for me to join Nick at The Savile Club in town for the Flyfishers' Dinner, where I would meet his friends, and then stay with him at St Michael's Manor in St Albans. Everything went according to plan until the last night in the hotel. I turned the bedside light out and received an almighty electric shock, which made me jump backwards with alarming speed. My unclad frame had not moved so fast for decades! I knocked my water, watch and glasses completely off the bedside table, soaking everything in range, but at least I did not fly across the room like one startled Collie dog I had heard about.

My beauty therapist, Jane, recalled that some time ago, she was on the telephone to her mother, when her mum suddenly announced: "I have to go now. The dog has just flown across the room!" Apparently, the Collie had bitten through the wire to the standard lamp and received an almighty shock, which had sent it into orbit.

Then, undaunted, Jane recounted another incident when she was babysitting for her daughter's baby son and all the lights fused. She noticed that the rest of the street still had power, so she cuddled her sobbing grandson and searched for the trip switches. No amount of switching restored the lights and no amount of searching found a candle or a torch, so she telephoned her daughter, who returned and undertook a little detective work. The culprit was found to be their trembling Jack Russell, Tiko, who had bitten through the cable to the washing machine and obviously received a nasty jolt, as his fur was still standing on end like a startled porcupine.

I invited my friend, Judy, to Devon for a few days rest and recuperation after a break with her boyfriend. The first morning was gloriously sunny, so we took William to Crow Point, to have a stretch before going to the kennels. As usual, I spoke to all the many dog-walkers to such an extent that Judy thought that I knew everyone in the locality. All the dogs, were well-behaved except for one particularly naughty male Goldie who reduced both of us (and his lady owner) to helpless laughter when he cocked his leg over her picnic basket! Thank goodness William was not the offender.

Later, we took William to Towsers kennels before our short Spring holiday in Cornwall. Judy and I stayed at The Old Custom House in Padstow, dining particularly well at Rick Stein's Café before visiting The Eden Project, The Lost Gardens of Heligan, Mevagissey, Port Isaac and Boscastle. On the way home we were scheduled to have lunch at Hoops Inn, near Horns Cross, but a fire-engine had beaten us there. Sadly, the thatched roof was on fire. We quickly changed our plans, drove past and had lunch at the Commodore before seeing the film *Marley and Me* in Barnstaple.

The film is very true to the book; Jennifer Anniston, Owen Wilson and the three children are exceptionally plausible, but it is the mischievous Marley who steals the show. He cavorts and leaps his way through the film as such a headstrong character that it is no surprise when he is banned from the dog-training classes. The film ends just as the book does, so I blubbed my way through it. My dry-eyed friend, an ardent tortoise fancier, handed me some tissues commenting heartlessly: "I would have got rid of the dog on Day One!"

People seem either to love dogs or hate them; there is no middle ground. For my next trip, I had arranged to visit Dorothy, an ardent dog-lover, and her Goldie, Daisy (William's girlfriend) in Surrey. I made sure that Daisy was not in season and prepared William for a long journey. En route, I spent two hours at the Nuffield Hospital, Taunton, for my morning clinic, making sure that the car was parked in the shade with the windows open and that it contained a large bowl of water for William. I asked two medical secretaries, who overlooked the car, to kindly keep an eye on my precious hound. Needless to say, there was a steady stream of medical staff fans visiting the good-looking star of *Barking Mad*. After the clinic, I took William for a walk in the adjoining park before driving to Surrey. On arrival, William was like an excited bull elephant ready to rampage right through the garden and into each of the adjoining properties; he bonded instantly with his female friend, who looked delicately feminine beside this brutish hulk.

He let off some of his pent up energy digging a hole in a recently turned over flower bed. This apparently was allowed, as long as he kept away from the newly barricaded vegetable garden, where Terry had just planted some seed potatoes. Dorothy and Terry's lovely daughter, Linsey, arrived with her beautiful daughters, Gemma and Charley, and their lively spaniel named Rooney. This dog loved Daisy. In fact, I was told that he was heavily protective of her, if another dog showed any interest. I could see trouble ahead, but even I did not anticipate what was about to happen.

Daisy's back legs became stuck in a piece of electric flex that was hanging from the back of the garage. William faced her and cleverly barked repeatedly for help. While Dorothy was setting Daisy free, Rooney flew at William's throat and a fight began, which was so alarming that I thought one of the animals would end up in smithereens. Linsey kicked Rooney away from William (twice) with her sheepskin boot and the tussle for Daisy's affection was halted. Surprisingly, the only injury was a gash to Rooney's neck, possibly from one of William's tusks.

The plan was to walk the three dogs on the common the

following day, while Linsey was working. I suggested that it would be better to walk them separately in view of the last debacle. So, reluctantly, Linsey agreed to walk Rooney before work. She then gathered up the children and they made their farewells. It was lovely to see them. Outside the house, Linsey looked blank for a minute, then said: "Where's my car?" To her horror, she spotted it down the hill on the opposite side of the road. She had forgotten to put on the handbrake and the car had rolled driverless down the road narrowly missing two parked cars, before mounting the pavement and demolishing a garden wall. Fortunately it had not ploughed into any motorists or pedestrians and, incredibly, no-one had seen it happen. On recollection, we remembered hearing a loud boom, but thought it was William hitting the metal waste bin with his tail!

The next day, Dorothy was going to drive the two dogs to the common in her car. Daisy jumped in, but William refused to move. We took Daisy out and William jumped in, but when Daisy jumped in, William jumped out. This silly act was repeated a number of times until we were helpless with laughter. It was like the 'wet and dry' couple, who only come out one at a time depending on the weather. Eventually, the dogs complied with our wishes and we set off for the common. Off the lead, they were so happy to be together. It was a lovely Spring day and a true joy to see the trees bearing their new pale-green leaves proudly guarding a carpet of wild pale-yellow primroses. William looked every inch the handsome male beside Daisy, who was a paler shade of cream and looked breathtakingly beautiful. They were a perfectly matched couple. Their progeny would amaze and astound Crufts.

After the walk, it was no surprise that William still defiantly refused to jump into Dorothy's car. If we manhandled him in, he would jump out when Daisy hopped in. We were laughing so much that another dog-walker asked if we needed help. This kind lady, Christine, lifted William in while I held his lead firmly from inside the car and eventually we were able to close the hatchback-door.

After lunch, Dorothy and I went into Guildford shopping, leaving the dogs in her garage for five hours. Having just seen the havoc that one dog can produce in a garage in the film

Marley and Me, and knowing that unfortunate events come in threes, we were anticipating a third calamity when we arrived home rather later than anticipated. The garage was un-touched; instead, two happy, sleepy dogs were curled up together. Dorothy and I let them out into the garden, fed them and popped them back into the garage while we had a very welcome glass of Merlot. Ten minutes later I popped my head into the garage. The third disaster had occurred.

There was white, fluffy kapok all over the garage floor, completely covering a very empty quilt cover, now disowned by both the excitable dogs. The monsters were thrown out into the garden, so that I could fill a large black bin-liner with diaphanous wads of stuffing. That evening, when we went to The Plough at Leatherhead for a delicious steak supper, we were exceedingly concerned as to the state of the garage when we arrived home. We need not have worried, the dogs were too exhausted from their long walk and subsequent pillow-fight to create any more mischief.

The next day I packed the car, thanked Dorothy for her wonderful hospitality and collected William. He refused to jump in. He did not want to leave Daisy. I trotted him in a circle and tried again. Nothing. Not a hop. Not even paws on the boot floor. Nothing. Exasperatingly, after the fourth attempt, I wrenched his paws onto the floor of the boot and lifted him in. He was coming home.

CHAPTER 3

NICK'S BIRTHDAY

Nick was scheduled to come down to Devon for Easter to celebrate his 60th birthday. Sadly, the previous Wednesday, we attended the funeral of Bryen Wood, a delightful and profoundly wise man, who had founded Bushey Museum. Bryen and Nick had both been passionate about the Museum and had worked tirelessly with others to promote, extend and organise the exhibits, until the Museum was a flourishing force in the village and surrounding area.

I took William to Towsers kennels and travelled by train to Reading station, where Nick met me and we went on to a smart hotel in Maidenhead for the night. The next morning, we attended a very sad service for Bryen at the Church of St James in Bushey. Jim gave a moving and eloquent tribute to Bryen, capturing the essence of his life with his lovely wife, June, and their family, before highlighting his involvement, total commitment and dedication to Bushey Museum. This local Museum is a living tribute to Bryen and all those involved in its inception, its present and its future. Bushey has strong links with the famous artist, Herkomer, his students and many other Bushey artists. Among the local artists, Lucy Kemp Welch is my particular favourite: I love the movement she has captured, using oil as a medium, where she has displayed horses that seem to thunder out of the picture.

Rather despondently, Nick and I left June and our friends and drove down to Devon, where the cottage felt empty and unloved without William. The next day we were reunited with an over-excited hound and our Easter break began. The weather smiled on us, so we visited Bovey Tracey and took William for a therapeutic walk along the river. Wills zig-zagged his way along the path dipping in and out of the River Bovey at every whim. He was wonderful company and great

17

fun to be with. The next day, we visited Crow Point, where William performed a series of acrobatic turns on the beach directly under our feet; the more we laughed, the more he flipped, until he resembled a sandy seal with limpid, thoroughly appealing, dark-brown eyes, designed to make us melt. This time the tears were coupled with laughter. It was such good therapy for us after the previously sad week.

Nick showed me an article in *The Daily Telegraph* describing a Golden Retriever from Poole, named Bailey, which underwent surgery to remove a tumour. The vet was astounded to find that the dog had eaten two golf balls, two rugby gloves, a mitten, a stocking and nine socks. Happily, Bailey made a full recovery. It's nice to think that Daily Telegraph readers must now be enlightened as to where all those odd socks go!

We visited Knightshayes Court in Tiverton, where we walked in the woods with Wills before visiting the stately home now owned by the National Trust. I was delighted to be able to use my NT membership card that my son, Martin, and daughter-in-law, Jo, had kindly given me for my birthday. I had popped it in the car ready for days like this. William was in his element; he was allowed to roam among the trees without a lead. He took a nose-dive into every speck of mud, until he was the colour of chocolate, but not nearly so tasty. We noticed that ALL the other dogs stayed clean. Obviously, 'proper dogs' did not!

We left him in the shade to congeal, while we had a light lunch, before visiting Wimbleball Lake, where we encouraged William to take the water. Amazingly, although he had never been interested in retrieving on dry land, he began to retrieve sticks in the lake while paddling, coming out to drop them for us. We returned home with a well-rinsed brute in a car smelling highly of wet dog. Later, my neighbour, John, astounded me by saying that our drinking water comes from that lake, so we stuck to bottled water (probably from the same source!), or something of a different colour and proof, for the rest of the week!

The next day Nick and I timed our visit to Lee Bay to coincide with low tide, so that we could walk around the rocks with Wills. The beach contained a plethora of rock pools, reached by a series of slippery stepping-stones. William was forever the sure-footed hound, while I was fearful that I would 'turn turtle' and break a number of important bones in my body by slipping on the slime and seaweed that coated the many stones. On reaching the sea through a crevice in the rocks, it was William's turn to be scared. He bounded backwards like a startled young penguin as each wave rolled gently in. This highly-bred hound could cope with mud, slime, sand and water, but became seriously alarmed by tiny rippling waves!

Nick and I visited Toby's Architectural Reclamation Centre, Fagin's Emporium and a number of Garden Centres looking for a suitable sculpture for Nick's garden in Ireland for his special birthday. I fancied giving him a bird bath, but he wanted one that was large enough for all the birds, that he regularly feeds, which probably wing in from the width of Ireland. We found nothing suitable, so Nick was charged with finding a large root-bound magnolia tree in Ireland and sending me the bill. It was to be planted in front of his kitchen window in his 'Grand Design' house, even though he had not yet taken up residence!

On Easter Sunday, I took Nick, Martin, Jo, Maggie and Charlie to dinner at the Penhaven Hotel at Parkham, where we enjoyed a wonderful celebratory evening for Nick's 60th. I shall never, EVER, forget the surprised and rather alarmed look on Nick's face when the hotel manager dimmed the lights and brought out a chocolate birthday cake, sporting four flaming candles, while the staff and fellow diners sang 'Happy Birthday'. They had expected it to be one of the little girls' birthdays! Immediately, in unison, my grand-daughters asked: "Please may we take the rest of the cake home?"

As we were leaving, a couple on the next table mentioned that their birthdays were in three day's time (not only were they born on the same day, but, amazingly, were the same age) These 'twins' thought that the children had behaved beautifully at a grown-up evening party. I puffed up in the kind of pride that grandparents enjoy. As the girls took the chocolate cake, carefully wrapped in silver foil, home, I thought: *"Nick will, forever, have fond memories of his special birthday!"*.

CHAPTER 4

OLD HILL FARM IN SPRING

Adelightful couple of men arrived to stay in the Barn
bringing with them a burst of summer sunshine. They
arrived in a small black car and, as if by magic,
unloaded the largest and most glorious German Shepherd
that I had ever seen. When I asked if this mountain lion was
friendly, I was told: "He does not like people or male dogs".
William and I quickly got the message! Suddenly, it was not
important to ask the brute's name; he was bigger than both of
us put together! I protected my pet by letting him out in the
garden only when the guests were at the seaside. I dead-
headed the hydrangeas and watered the garden while they
were out. When they returned, William and I quickly
retreated into the house. On seeing this giant through the
kitchen window, Wills went for the jugular with a jumping-
jack routine, protecting me by barking bravely, while he
himself was safe behind the glass. I stayed inside until the
hairy monster was firmly tucked up into the Barn.

William has settled down to be a wonderful companion,
who knows the rules, even though, like children, he tries to
stretch them to fit his needs. He will sit and wait for his meal
until allowed to eat and he will stay in the kitchen and only
mount three stairs to his favourite resting place. He will come
when called, though I still give him a biscuit each time he
complies. It was comical when I was staying at Dorothy's. Her
dog, Daisy, would only go out if she had a biscuit, while
William would only come in if he was given one! When
walking, he considers my heel to be a yard in front of me, but
the lead is slack, so I am happy. All things considered, he is
the perfect pup. Until.............

We walked down the lane from my cottage and heard
bleating coming from the very top of one of the six-foot high

Devon hedges. There, on the very top, was a tiny lost lamb struggling to stand firm and pitifully crying for help. William leapt to the rescue by bounding six feet in the air with me still attached to his kite string. The lamb was totally surprised and immediately sprang back into the field. Eventually, William settled down from seeking other lambs who might require his mighty presence, so that we were able to continue our walk. When we returned, we saw that the unscathed lamb had been happily reunited with its mother; for Wills, a job well done. Perhaps William should add sheep-herding to his growing number of skills. After all, one should start with something small and gradually work up to the stocky flock.

The next day, I walked William down the lane and noticed that his ears had pricked up and his head had become airborne like a helium balloon. Through the high Devon hedge, he could hear the farmer whistling to his sheep-dog in the adjoining field. Between them, they were rounding up the sheep and lambs in preparation for a mystery ride in a rickety trailer. It amazed me how every time the farmer whistled, William moved to one side of the lane, and when he called "Come by" he moved the other way. No doubt, over the years, farmers have found the whistles and words that dogs inherently understand. I was full of wonder that a dog, who had only ever heard a cautionary "Aa Aa" when he spied lambs through the five-barred gates, could understand and adhere to commands that he had never heard before. Perhaps he had a natural inborn talent for rounding up sheep!

I feared for the lambs' safety. One of my neighbours, who was out walking on his own, as his dog had sadly died, reported a sighting of a large male fox, the kind that could easily devour a baby lamb before breakfast. There is also an abundance of bunnies merrily hopping and skipping over the neighbouring fields and, when William is safely inside, dancing on my lawn. One time, I counted two adult rabbits and four babies nibbling in unison, before they were joined by a pair of ducks who were misguided enough to think that I had a pond. This year, I hit on the idea of clapping my hands loudly (noise travels well between the two hills either side of my cottage) prior to letting William out to thunder down the garden. This simple action (why had I not thought of it before?) has spared the rabbit population, but sends the predator crazy. I love seeing them hopping about in the wild, though I have been known to pop into the pet shop just to see the tame rabbits! The lop-eared, very furry ones are my favourites and even though I cannot get close enough to stroke them, just seeing them goes someway to satisfying my inborn love of fur.

I chose a Goldie because they have such wonderful coats. 'His Furriness' is a joy to stroke, nuzzle and play with. Once a day, he stands eagerly while I comb him to prevent him from moulting all over the floor, but even so, in warm weather, he surreptitiously discards large chunks of unwanted fur under the kitchen table, which swirl around every time the door is opened. I guess if I was wearing a (fake) fur coat, I would want to take it off during the summer months, but I would hang it up, not leave it spread out on the kitchen floor!

I needed a fur coat when the early sunny spring weather took a nose-dive, bringing ferocious winds that would have been more suitable in an Arctic winter. I decided this was not a day for the faint-hearted and curled up with a book that Nick had kindly bought me. It was titled *One Dog at a Time* and written by Pen Farthing ('Penny Farthing' to his mates!), a Sergeant in the Royal Marines serving in Now Zad, a town in Helmand Province. It recounted, with much sensitivity, how Pen provided sanctuary for a number of stray dogs in a makeshift pound, including one fighting dog with docked ears, docked tail and a wire collar, which he had bravely released from a barbed-wire road barrier. The story portrayed not just how these gallant men cared for dogs that sought refuge within their camp, but how the dogs created a diversion, a reason for living, during the inhumane raids and ambushes from the Taliban. It was a gripping account and a recommended read.

Over a pub supper in the Chichester Arms, I told Glennis about these dogs, which were bred to fight in Afghanistan. She commented that dog-fights were still taking place in some out-of-the-way places in Devon, often with big money involved. I was appalled that this practise was current, but more shocked to think that it happened locally. In the pub, we met the local farmer accompanied by his beautiful Siberian Huskie. He said that William was the only dog who barked at his dog and that he found it irritating. Whenever William is outside barking, I bring him in, as sound travels extraordinarily well in the vicinity. When I mentioned that I regularly heard his dog howling in the evening, he commented: "That's what wolves do!"

Martin and Jo left my grand-daughters, Maggie and Charlie, with me while they were stocking their garden from St John's Garden Centre. I encouraged Martin to take his hound, Bob, with him as I was unable (unwilling) to look after two grand-children and two over-excitable dogs! I lit a fire from all the carpenter's end-cuts of wood, and Maggie, Charlie and I cuddled up on the sofa together, so that they could read their new Ladybird books to me. They read simple sentences to me about Peter and Jane and later about Pat, the dog. I was most impressed by their grasp of reading, so after each page I clapped my hands heartily, out of all proportion to the task involved, but it created some giggles and encouraged these young readers to enjoy attaining such an important skill.

I read later that dogs like William may be able to help little children to read. According to *The Daily Telegraph*, pupils in a Primary School in Bournemouth were encouraged to read out loud to dogs. It was stated that the dogs did not laugh if the novice readers stuttered or stumbled over their words. The dogs were rewarded in kind with pleasurable stroking. I reminisced back to the first time that I gave a speech, many years ago, when the new Physiotherapy Department was opened at BUPA Hospital Bushey. I practised in front of Oscar, my white Persian cat, who quickly became fed up, lifted his magnificent tail and left the room. So as Physiotherapy Manager, I commenced my virgin speech by revealing details of my home-practice technique, and invited my audience to leave if they became as bored as Oscar!

I went to bed thinking of 'Peter likes Jane' and 'Jane likes Pat' and fell deeply asleep. I was woken abruptly by William barking himself hoarse at around midnight. Occasionally there were flashes, but no thunder. I peeped cautiously through each window in turn for possible intruders, wondering what on earth I would do if I saw anyone. I was totally puzzled and rather alarmed, but I pacified my best friend and settled back to bed. An hour later, there was more insistent barking, so we went through the same security procedure all over again. The next day I asked John, my neighbour, if he had heard anything suspicious. He informed me that it was probably the farmer shooting rabbits or foxes and that I must have seen flashes from the firearm.

I always feel more secure when I have visitors, so it was a pleasure to collect my friend, Mary, from Tiverton Station prior to our visit to France. It had been a busy day. I had risen early so that I could oversee my carpenter, Dave and my gardener, Barry, replacing the furniture in my Conservatory after the floor had been sealed. This was the last part of the 2009 Conversion, a project that had started when the lilac was in bloom last year and had finished as the lilac was resplendent again. Dave was going on holiday to Woolacombe, so I gave him a bottle of wine and a copy of 'Barking Mad in Barnstaple' with the inscription: "To Dave, Thank you for all your hard work in all weathers making my house so beautiful, Grace". He was more delighted with the book than the wine, as he was looking forward to some light-hearted holiday reading. I then dashed to an emergency appointment with my lovely dentist to have my smart new crown filed down, so that I could chew more happily. From there, I went to the Tarka Tennis Centre for an enjoyable couple of hours of indoor tennis with my friends, before a dash to the station to meet Mary.

As the weather was cold and wet, I lit the fire and made Mary a cup of tea in the sitting room before collecting my post. In it, was the contract from Steve Pugsley at Halsgrove to sign for my new book *William – Still Barking*. I popped the post on the kitchen table and said to Mary that I was going over to my office in the barn to check and sign the contract. William was ahead of me. He removed the post from the table, scattered some cheques over the drive and disappeared into the garden, at the speed of a furtive fox, to devour the contract! I shouted. I chased him. I yelled: "Sit!." Eventually, I was able to prise a soggy, dog-eared contract from William's mouth. Certainly, it was his book and maybe even his contract, but I learned yet another lesson on not leaving anything within reach of my attack hound.

CHAPTER 5

'LES GIRLS' IN FRANCE

With a heavy heart, I left William at Towsers Kennels in preparation for a visit to Brittany to stay with my good friends, John and Ann. Mary, who was the Theatre Manager at BUPA Hospital Bushey when I was the Physiotherapy Manager, was accompanying me on the flight from Exeter to Brest. We were collected from the new rather impressive Brest Airport building by John and Ann and driven to their beautiful house in Lanfains, a little hamlet South of Quintin. Alphonse, their friendly dog, was waiting at a dog-sized upstairs window for us to appear, before rushing downstairs for the many strokes on offer. He had either forgotten about the time when he was hit by a car while I was walking him two years ago, or he chose to ignore it, in order to receive his aforementioned fondles. Every time I cosseted Alphonse, I missed William. A week without Wills was a long time. It was lovely taking 'Phonse for a walk (never again on my own!), but I wished that I could have walked with William too.

Mary, Ann and I walked round the beautiful lake at Bosméléac with Alphonse, keeping the lake on the right, promising to walk round backwards next time to capture the reverse view! The next day 'Phonse was grounded, while we joined the local villagers at a large refectory table for a delicious long French lunch at l'Hermitage-Lorges. The afternoon was lost to a sound sleep, which swiftly followed a feeling of lethargy brought on by an inherent ability to relax, and of course had nothing to do with any alcohol that I may have consumed.

I felt well-rested the next day and ready for a girly shopping trip to St Brieuc. The colourful market was decked with a plethora of eye-catching trinkets, which appealed to our aesthetic sides, so we each bought French necklaces from a stall holder, who announced that she was related, many generations back, to Cartier. Our 'Cartier' necklaces cost 3 Euros each and our shopping trip commenced once we had started spending. We all bought trendy grey linen jackets; each buying a different shade, size and shape! We visited every (yes, every) children's shop to buy a cute dress for Charlie's fifth birthday and a similar dress in a different colour for Maggie, as it was not her birthday! A good deal of time and trouble was spent on the careful selection, as many pretty dresses were outrageously expensive, possibly due to the poor exchange rate. We then collapsed at a table in the square for lunch, where we sat outside watching some International students busily making an action film. In the evening, Mary and I took our hosts to Hotel du Commerce in Quintin, the best restaurant in town, for a delicious dinner.

The next day, I started pining for William as 'les girls' walked along the Rigole d'Huilverne canal with Alphonse. This waterway runs along the river making a particularly spectacular walk. The trees with their light green feathery leaves whispered as they rippled in the breeze, thoughtfully protecting the carpet of pale yellow flowers that miraculously peeped out to cheer our spirits and herald the spring. Wills would have been in his element; he would have sunk into the black mud alongside the river and covered himself entirely, starting with his nose, painting his paws and quickly working up to include his whole body. Only his fluffy tail would have been spared. He would have been in paradise. I made a 'note to self' not to leave the UK, in future, without him.

The following day we visited Plaine-Haute to see a sale of Brochante. There were no antiques on sale of interest, only some tacky second-hand gear. In the afternoon, we tried and failed to find a walk among boulders along the River Gouet. Another note to self: take Wills and a detailed map next time!

As so often happens in France, tourist attractions and shops have an unhappy knack of being shut on the day of the visit. Therefore, it was absolutely no surprise to find the stunning Abbé du Bon-Repos (the home of a spectacular Son et Lumiére on certain dates of the calendar) sadly closed. We swiftly moved on and consoled ourselves with a crêpe lunch (with chips!) overlooking a white van obscuring a magnificent view of the Lac de Guerledan, which connects to the Nante-Brest canal. After lunch we were amazed to find the linen museum at the pretty village of St Théla open. We gave the museum an 'admission-fee-related' miss, but enjoyed browsing through all the delightful items in the shop, until we saw the prohibitive prices.

Our week in France sadly came to an end, when the day arrived, all too quickly, for our return. Ann and John had been perfect hosts; we had enjoyed a week of wonderful spring weather; we had completed *The Times* crossword by lunchtime each day; and had walked Alphonse into the ground, leaving him able only to croon comically to *Britain's Got Talent* on the television! Apparently, this musical dog has a preference for the church music in *Songs of Praise*, though his all time favourite is *God Save the Queen*! John drove us back to Brest Airport hours before our flight, as I have an irrational fear of missing a flight. Needless to say, Mary and I sat waiting in the airport lounge for so long that we were the last people to board!

Back to earth on a Sunday evening, we found Tescos closed and no food in the 'fridge or wine in the 'cellar', so we had scotch eggs from the garage for supper, which compared unfavourably with Ann's fabulous cooking and John's abundant supply of wine. I started a diet.

The very next day, I collected Wills from Towsers.

"Has he behaved himself?" I asked.

"Why do you always ask that?" Sean replied. "He always behaves himself when he is here."

I paid £100 in kennel fees and took my precious cargo home.

CHAPTER 6

IRISH INTERLUDE

William and I were reunited. I gave him more walks and went on a diminishing diet. Just as I was about to become supremely fit, I noticed, in my diary, that I had to leave my pal and with him my exercise programme and present a lecture in the Conference Centre at Wyboston Lakes for the Association of Acupuncture Chartered Physiotherapists.

The night before I left home, Wills was moaning at my bedroom door at 5.30am. He knew that he was not allowed upstairs, but he had never moaned like this before. He sounded in pain. I led him downstairs where he indicated that he wanted to go outside. I took him outside to pee, which took much longer than usual. He then came back inside before depositing doggy diarrhoea on the kitchen floor. I cleared up the offending mess, realised why he was acting strangely, gave him a hug and hopped back into bed. The next morning, I took him reluctantly to Springfield Kennels.

At the Conference, my lecture titled *'Under Every Good Man...........'* was very well received by 200 physiotherapy delegates, mainly I think because, early on, I said "The centre of gravity is at the penis" instead of saying "The centre of gravity is at the pelvis"! I possibly made the situation worse by adding: "I don't know why I said that". From then on, I had a captive audience, who seemed intent on listening for my next unfortunate turn of phrase and who readily appreciated a repeat of my Professorial lecture. I left the conference to travel the 262 miles back home to Devon.

The next day, when I collected Wills, John announced that his stools had been loose (William's not John's). By now, I had worked out that I had given Wills some Bresaola beef before I went away, because the sell-by date was looming. Then, John told me that some dog-owners empty the 'fridge into the dog bowl before they go on holiday. Thus, I learned another lesson on dog-feeding etiquette prior to a kennel stay.

After just three days at home with Wills, I was scheduled to present a Female Continence Study Day to a group of physiotherapists in Dublin. Lovingly, I explained to my best friend that he would be staying with his pals at Springfield Kennels again. I drove up and opened the hatchback. William refused to jump out. He lay down in the boot and curled up determinedly, looking up at me with his deep-brown watery eyes underlined with those ever-appealing white crescents. How could I ignore this behaviour? I cuddled him and told him that he was going to have a ball. This defiant down-in-the –mouth behaviour had never happened before. I felt guilty beyond belief. He had always leapt into the kennels without so much as a tearful goodbye or even a backward glance. John tried to coax him out of the car without success, so he cleverly decided to send for Ella, a black Labrador bitch. Ella worked her magic. Once William spied his girlfriend, he leapt out of the car like a bee on heat and chased her deep into the field, while I mused that there would be many days ahead when I would want to 'Send for Ella'!

After the Study Day in Dublin, Nick took me for a mini-holiday to Donegal, where we experienced the ragged beauty of the ancient granite hills bordering several misshapen lakes, only surpassed by the majestic coastline, where the spiky hills slashed their way into the sea. The ocean was as volatile as the weather, as it swept repeatedly over the jagged rocks piercing the bay to produce a spray of snow-white foam and ruptured surf. We took refuge from the drizzle in a delightful shop in Ardara, which produced fine Irish tweed. While Nick was discussing the possibilities of having a roll of tweed custom-made to his own colour-palette for curtains, I tried on a number of short jackets. It was amazing how different colours either complemented or drained my weather-beaten complexion. I left the shop with a beautiful dark green suit and matching scarf in the finest, lightest tweed, with a view to smartening myself up when I am lecturing.

The next day we had an appointment to see a property at Mullaghmore in County Sligo with breathtaking views of the harbour in the foreground stretching to the beautiful hills of Donegal in the distance. Nick wanted to buy this house to renovate for a second home. It was a former nun's home, containing a maze of ten sad, single bedrooms, each containing a dusty sculpture or faded picture of the Virgin Mary. Unhappily, this religious sanctuary had received no upgrading or redecoration since the early Sixties. It was as if, during the decades of tranquillity and abstention, the clock had stopped and time in this convent house had silently stood still. We wondered where the nuns had gone; had they been relocated elsewhere or had their numbers sadly dwindled in the passage of time with no new postulant recruitment?

After a wonderful break, I returned home, flying from Dublin to Exeter before rushing straight to the kennels to collect young William. He had enjoyed his parties with Ella, though he far preferred – oh deary-dear – to romp with a male sheepdog! He received a favourable report from John, who seemed to be increasingly fond of my large brute. Just before I left, I met a couple who were collecting their eight-month-old male retriever and moaning that they had to lift him into the car. I recalled that William only jumped into the boot himself when he was one year old following a visit to a French vet! "Yes", the lady said. "I read that in *Barking Mad*!"

Nick was lucky to win his long-drawn-out bidding war for the convent house in Mullaghmore. He had grand ideas for this unique property, which involved the builders, who had almost finished his house overlooking Lough Sheelin (just the dog kennel to complete now). These builders would seamlessly move from one job to the next to start removing the floors and generally gutting the place, before rebuilding the nunnery into a grand four-bedroom holiday home. I was delighted. William would be able to walk across the road to the beach and frolic in the adjoining sand-dunes. I have always been frightened about the adders in the sand-dunes at Braunton Burrows and Saunton Sands so I have kept William well-away from these areas. Fortunately, thanks to St Patrick, there are no snakes in Ireland, so he can frequent the dunes without any danger.

I was cleaning the new barn bedroom, which overlooks the garden, when I saw a snake wiggling its way purposely across my lawn. As William was outside, I immediately assumed the role of 'brave protector' and rushed over to the offending reptile, in order to prevent my hound from being bitten. The beast was about two feet long and an inch wide with a mottled-brown appearance. I was concerned that it might have been another adder. I had seen a metre-long adder with silver and black zig-zag markings snaking across my drive two years ago, so ever since have been fearful that it (or one of its offspring) would return. Whenever I go to bed, I always lift the duvet and go snake-spotting before I jump in. I am not sure what Freud would have made of this! Would it have had sexual connotations or would he have linked my fear to my earliest childhood memory? I can remember sitting in my pram, which was parked in the summer house, which my father had built at the end of the garden. If I cried (possibly because I was abandoned at the bottom of the garden!), a neighbour would poke her finger through a knot-hole in the wooden fence and wiggle it up and down. This kept me entertained for hours – maybe even days.

I searched the web for pictures of British snakes. I discovered that this new intruder could be a grass snake and reach a whopping five feet in length. Fortunately these chaps are not venomous, so there is no danger to dogs (or indeed to me). I read that grass snakes can lay 40 eggs each spring, so I am expecting to see an army of them any day now! They live in piles of dead and decaying plant material, taking sustenance from flavoursome frogs and tasty toads, so I can see why they have found my rotting compost heap at the bottom of my garden to be an ideal habitat. I should have been re-assured by the information provided on the web, but forever, I will err on the side of caution and treat every wriggling creature as an adder – just in case I identified it incorrectly!

The grass snake slid smoothly away under the blackberry bushes to greet the rest of his or her extended family, while I returned to my cottage. As I was walking up the drive, I saw a very dead sparrow lying on its back in a flower bed with its curled claws pointing upwards. I picked it up by its tail to fling it over the hedge. As I took a backswing, William pounced and ran off with the poor little bird in his mouth. I never found the bird again and can only imagine that William had the audacity to swallow it whole.

CHAPTER 7

THE LONG HOT SUMMER

My friend, Lyn came down again to stay with me for the weekend, accompanied by Cassie, her loyal ten-year-old Boxer. This lovely dog was fighting fit for her age, despite having had corneal graft surgery to one eye, a dry and cracked nose and irregular patches of fur-loss over her back. The weekend weather was predicted to be glorious and it certainly did not disappoint. With much difficulty, I stood perilously on the garden table and erected the sunshade for the first time of the year, so that we could enjoy breakfast, lunch and dinner outside each day. On Sunday night, I lit a barbecue and kept the dogs inside for fear of losing the precious fillet steak when our backs were turned. Both dogs played, ate and slept well together. Cassie shared Will's dried dog food, as Lyn had forgotten to bring her dog's moist meaty chunks. Cassie must have objected to this, as once finished, she moved forwards and peed in her bowl! Well, mostly in her bowl, but enough mess to register her disgust!

We decided not to travel in a hot car that weekend. The temperature was 81 degrees Fahrenheit, so it was far too hot to take our fur-coated animals to the beach. Instead, we took them down the hill to walk along the shady Tarka trail by the river. William made a nose-dive into the muddy ditch bordering the river and ran his nose determinedly forward like a plough, so that he became progressively more discoloured and unsavoury, until he turned into a black panther. His pleasure was heightened by the raw delight of shaking excess mud over each of us in turn. In contrast, and rather maddeningly, Cassie behaved like a pristine princess. She was just not interested in muck or mud, but kept herself clean as a pea in a whistle. It was a surprise to both of us that neither dog was interested in cooling off (or in William's case, cleaning off) in the river, as this had been part of our plan.

Lyn walked back up the hill with a shining brown boxer, while I lead a mucky, muddy muffin, who was as ecstatic as Larry on happy pills.

After Cassie had been taken back home to Bristol, William lay on his stomach and stretched out his long legs to all points of the compass in a most ungainly pose. He was well and truly spent after his excitement with Cassie, but mainly because the weather was so alarmingly hot for humans and animals, bald or furry. My old stone and cob cottage does not overheat in Summer, so I was delighted to find I had a reading job to attend to, which I could undertake in the cool of the drawing room. The proofs for *William; Still Barking* had arrived from the publisher, so I needed to do a little proof-reading. My legs turned to jelly out of raw excitement! I am unable to explain this phenomenon, but it happened before *Barking Mad in Barnstaple* was published. I wobbled to the sofa at 2pm with a glass of cold water and a pink pen (red is too critical) and proceeded to read and make the odd helpful (I hoped) correction.

I started reliving my life over the last year and thoroughly enjoyed reading about my increasingly better-behaved pal. As I turned the pages, I started to become prouder and prouder of my mutt. As I continued to read, I was totally transfixed. He had grown from a crazy puppy into a fine male dog in the space of a year. His behaviour had improved out of all recognition from the wilfully disobedient hound that so exasperated me, into a wonderfully loveable companion. True, he still had spirit, but that 'joie de vivre' was part of his unpredictable character, which was rather endearing.

Nick telephoned and disturbed me from my enjoyable task. My watch had stopped earlier in the day, as it needed a new battery.

"What time is it?" I asked him.

"Seven o'clock," he replied. I had been thoroughly absorbed with my reading for five hours without a break! After a shorter than usual telephone call, I rushed to take William out for his walk and gave him a late supper. Then it hit me! While I was reading all about my pet, I had neglected him. I felt ashamed. Why had he not barked for attention? Perhaps dogs do have a sixth sense and know when silence assists their route to stardom.

Nick invited my star (and me) to Ireland for the first two weeks of August. This posed a problem. Being a wimp, I needed to lie down on the ferry, as I suffer from mal-de-mer. The only sailings with cabins that operated during the day were from Holyhead to Dublin. The Swansea to Cork sailings had been temporarily discontinued until 2010 and the Fishguard to Dublin ferry was sadly cabin-less. As the hike from Devon up to Holyhead would take forever, I trawled the internet to find a dog-friendly hotel near the ferry port. I found a Travelodge at Holyhead for just £50 for the night plus £17 for young Wills. I quickly booked the hotel prior to the outward journey and again for the return trip. I envisaged using my 'Tom Tom' satellite navigation system, which Martin and Jo had kindly given me for Christmas, to find Nick's new house. I had visited his house many times over the past six years, but had never driven in Ireland, as he had always kindly met me from Dublin Airport.

Six years ago during an Irish holiday we had found his derelict house waiting, longingly, to be restored. It provided truly breathtaking views of Lough Sheelin, when we peered through the cracks in the grubby rear windows. Eventually, planning consent was granted for a 'Grand Design' house, with spectacular glass windows spanning the whole of the aspect overlooking the lake. After a lifetime of waiting, designing, waiting, organising, waiting, sourcing, waiting, snagging and yet more waiting, the house was ready for Nick to move in. The residence was finished to a high specification by an Irish builder named Declan, and his band of workers. Unfortunately, some of the Poles in the workforce had hopped back to Poland before the building was completed, causing further delays. I had sent Nick a card wishing him 'Good Luck in Your New Home' months before, when I came across a card, which I considered to be perfect, sporting a tortoise moving into his new abode! There was no provision for a tortoise or two in this grand house, but there was a pad for young Wills. Nick had cleverly constructed a custom-made kennel and exercise area leading to an outside hot and cold shower at dog height! Everything had been thoughtfully designed to perfection. It was ready for William.

Obviously, Nick was expecting the muffin to perform true to type. He had seen how sandy he becomes within a few minutes on the beach. He knew about his desire to frequent dirty ditches and mucky mulch, so he hoped that he would be one step ahead of this hopelessly mud-loving hound.

William had dug a hole in my beautiful hydrangea bed, which went someway to explain why frequently he returned from the garden with a very grubby nose. The hole had started life as a rabbit hole and Wills decided to enlarge it, to see who was at home. He made one mistake. He failed to let me know what he was doing. One day in a fit of enthusiasm, I decided to extract the waist-high nettles, thistles and dock leaves from the bed behind the barn. I pulled on my rubber boots and happily filled three wheel-barrow loads with weeds, before taking them down to the end of the garden to throw over my snake-pit. All went well until I walked through the mature hydrangea bed to admire my work, when suddenly, without warning, I disappeared down the said rabbit-hole. Fortunately, I did not twist my ankle or arrive in Wonderland, but it was rather a shock. I hoped the rabbit (white?) had moved home before this incident, otherwise he may have been very late.

Dogs are descended from wolves, who dig tunnels as shelter from the elements, in order to get a good night's rest. Martin Clunes recounts in his book *A Dog's Life* how both his Cocker Spaniels and his Labrador shared many similar characteristics, such as 'fighting for rank' and 'having a pecking order for food', with their dingo and wolf ancestors. Martin even went up to the Wildlife and Dinosaur Park at Combe Martin and entered the enclosure of wolves with Shaun, the keeper. Certainly these wild animals had been bred in captivity, but I would not have been so foolhardy. I had seen a programme on television where this extraordinary 'wolf-man' had received a severely gashed cheek from the claws of one of these dangerous creatures. I wondered if this incident occurred before or after Doc Martin's visit. If he had previously seen the programme, he may not have been so brave.

Fortunately, I was out when the mighty bullocks broke out from the field adjoining my cottage, leaving a bull-sized hole in the hedge. I say fortunately, as this is the lane that I use to walk William at least twice a day. I cannot imagine the mayhem that would have occurred if we had been confronted by a herd of frisky bullocks. It is best not to envisage the scenario. Suffice it to say that I would have been scared out of my skin and possibly unable to control myself or my hound. Obviously, the bullocks were shit scared, as the newly tarred and stoned lane was covered in sloshy-brown poo-pats. We have sheep escaping at regular intervals, due to poor maintenance of the Devon hedges, but rarely do we have large livestock making a bid for freedom. The last bulls to leave their pastures crashed through two hedges to make a surprise visit to the cows in the neighbouring field. The farmer was not as delighted as the cows or, indeed, the bulls, who stubbornly refused to return home.

I told Nick about the bullocks. This was his advice, based on years of walking through fields, when out salmon fishing: "Do not run away or they will stampede. If a bull comes towards you, touch it on the nose and he will be more frightened of you than you are of him (impossible!). It does help to have a fishing rod in one hand, as you can use it for that purpose. Take a walking stick with you, when you walk down the lane, as this will do the trick."

Dear reader, can you just imagine trying to tap each one of a herd of escaped bullocks, on the nose and getting a hit every time? How would Wills have reacted? Would he assist with the nose-poking or simply flee? The elephant-sized hole in the hedge was mended the next day with flimsy wire fencing and a slither of barbed wire, which appeared totally inadequate, so I boycotted the lane until the meadow was filled with sheep again. Then I considered my situation in the country. I was living between snakes and bulls, but I would not go back to Chesham Bois for anything. I loved my life here in Devon with William.

The area of North Devon in which I reside, surrounding the estuary of the Taw and Torridge Rivers, was designated by UNESCO in 2002 as a World Class Biosphere Reserve. It aims to discover how people can enjoy a high quality of life based upon a superb natural environment. The website states: "About 53,000 people live in the biosphere reserve, who are mainly engaged in services, manufacturing, agriculture and fishing. Braunton Burrows Biosphere Reserve is a site where traditional land use practices are still maintained today. Grazing by Soay sheep and cattle on saltmarshes was practiced for more than a century and still maintains the marshes in a condition suitable for wintering wildfowl. Traditional local fishery harvests Atlantic salmon sea trout and sea bass, which are species that rely on the site as part of their lifecycle. Also mussel fishery and the harvest of ulva and laver are still practiced in a traditional way."

By way of an oversight, it failed to mention any local vicious vipers or belligerent bulls!

CHAPTER 8

VISITORS

A lovely young couple, named Ben and Karen, arrived with Molly the mongrel, to spend a week's holiday in the Barn. They brought with them the most glorious weather, which they imagined (hoped?) would last the week. While they were down the lane exploring the Tarka Trail, I decided to freshen up the hydrangeas in the Barn garden and water the lavender in tubs bordering my cottage, with the hose carefully set to sprinkle. This resulted in two adverse events. Firstly, before I could safely tuck the hosepipe away, a black cloud drifted over the Barn and emptied itself over the garden. The second unexpected side-effect to watering my flowers was all too evident the next morning. When I looked in the mirror, I was greeted by a very sunburned face, with a nose that made me look like a highly-painted inebriated gnome.

Hey ho! Before I went off to work (sans shovel), I let William meet Molly. He was intrigued. He teased her with a series of exploratory greeting sniffs followed by some rather comical reverse-thrust-with-twist bunny-jumps, learned from the little chaps who share the lawn. His stance and demeanour were that of a supremely confident dog, thoroughly at home in his own skin. He seemed to be looking down on this new arrival. I do not think that it was a class thing (pedigree versus mongrel snootiness), but more an inequality of size. William stood majestically, like the king of the pride, who was stronger and more powerful than the rest of the lion world. And he was on his own territory. No-one messed with Wills.

No-one except the elements! The next day, the heaviest cloud-burst on record funnelled directly over my property. I have never seen water pouring down so determinedly, since I visited Niagara Falls. I called Wills inside, just before the lightning heralded an electric storm. I have never seen

William so agitated. He followed me upstairs to a floor which he knew was out of-bounds and trembled against my legs. He was unfazed by the roar of the thunder; but each time there was a startling flash, he recoiled in abject terror. No amount of stroking and comforting helped to calm him down, until the storm moved on as quickly as it had arrived, taking with it the frightening lightning flashes.

The next flashes of brilliance to arrive came in the shape of my two grand-daughters, Maggie aged six years and Charlie aged five years. They were coming to stay the night, while Martin and Jo were helping to recruit interest in their Beach-Cleaning Programme at the festival in Croyde. The children arrived with little pink suitcases-on-wheels, packed to the brim with everything that they could possibly need. I took them to Crow Point, so that we could walk William. This was the first time that I had walked William with my grand-children on my own, so I was anxious to see if I could manage it. I chose a beach where William could run free straight from the car, so that I did not have to hold two little hands and one lead. I sun-creamed the children and insisted they wore their new sunhats. They equally insisted that they wore their sun-glasses, so sufficiently plastered and protected, we set off.

We met a lady who had gathered a bucket of samphire from the beach. Eagerly, we searched for this delicacy at the water's edge, but without any luck. She had picked all the new shoots, leaving none for us to take home and try. Nonetheless, the outing was successful for Wills, who entertained us by alternately nosing his way through the sea before rolling in the sand.

When we arrived at the car, Maggie tearfully announced that she had lost her sun-glasses, so we popped a sandy, sea-drenched William in the car, before trying to retrace our tracks, while scanning the beach for something pink. This was an almost impossible mission, as the beach was vast and we had walked a fair way across it. Suddenly, I stepped on something that cracked underfoot. At the same time, Maggie shouted: "My sun-glasses!" It was a miracle to find the glasses, but such extraordinarily bad luck to tread on them. What chances were there of finding anything on this vast beach, and, even more, what was the chance of stepping on the one thing that you were looking for?

"I'm so sorry," I said, hurriedly. "I'll buy you some more." Maggie was still tearful when she told me that her Daddy had bought them in London and that he would mend them for her. Then, she assumed the adult role and said: "Gran Gran, why didn't you look where you were walking"!

The next day was a beautifully sunny day. The kind of glorious summer day that I was pleased to share with my next visitors. I took Alan, my brother, and Rosemary, my sister-in-law, to the same beach and told them how we miraculously found Maggie's sunglasses among all the sand and pebbles. We also found many samphire shoots popping up all over the shore-line, but had arrived ill-equipped to harvest these delicacies, as we were sadly bucket-less. We walked all round the Point, sinking into the sand in most places, which stretched our leg muscles from their bony attachments. When we saw Lundy Island and Hartland Point, I announced that it was time to turn round and head back to the car.

William had been perfect and a joy to be with, so very different from the time when I took him as a young puppy to visit my brother in Dorset and he (the puppy, not Alan) rolled in every bit of available mud, leaving me with the unenviable task of lifting this hyperactive grubby mutt into the boot of my car. This time, he washed himself dutifully in the sea, before jumping back into the car and gulping down a bowl full of water. I asked Alan if this was their usual length of walk. My fitter, older brother replied: "We usually walk 12 miles"!

Before I received my next visitors, I had to teach 33 Portuguese physiotherapists how to provide conservative treatment for men with incontinence and erectile dysfunction. Reluctantly (and with a large helping of guilt), I left Wills at Towsers Kennels and dashed up to Bristol airport. Eventually, after queuing in the heat for about three days, I boarded the shuttle bus to take me to the plane, so I was highly delighted when a tall young man kindly gave me his seat. I sat down and, to my horror, immediately realised that the seat was sopping wet. I leapt up, imagining that the previous incumbent had experienced severe uncontrollable bladder problems. I had to sit on my wet skirt (and wet pants) for 2 hours on the flight to Lisbon, smelling highly of urine. I felt so embarrassed and could not wait to wash myself, my skirt and my underwear (avoid seat 3A on EasyJet). Although this was a ghastly experience, it provided a realistic insight into the sort of stresses that some of my patients cope with on a daily basis, and illustrated exactly why I had dedicated my working life to helping men and women to achieve bladder control and with it, a restoration of confidence.

On arrival in the searing heat of Lisbon, I had to queue for about an hour at passport control, long enough for Fatima's husband, Jill, who was kindly meeting me, to think that I had missed the flight. I arrived with swollen ankles, which reduced in a couple of hours after I forsook the beach in favour of sitting on the bed with my feet elevated. The next day, the ankle swelling returned after the day's lectures and then again following the queues at booking in, immigration and passport control before the two-hour flight home. When people say: "You have been to Portugal, how lovely." I have to bite my tongue until it is almost amputated.

The glorious summer weather continued and brought my close friends, Judy and Kate to stay. They admired my new conversion works on the obligatory 'conducted tour', which culminated in me proudly giving them each their own new 'en suite bedroom'. The sky was wonderfully blue on the first day, so we took William to visit Crow Point, where we covered ourselves with sun cream and enjoyed a large helping of Continental weather. Wills followed us closely, not wanting to miss out on the fun, unless there was a sandy puddle that was much too inviting to ignore. My sand-caked monster crashed out later, while we watched Andy Murray win a five-set match on his way to glory at Wimbledon.

The next day we visited Saunton Sands and were delighted to find that this breathtakingly beautiful beach was almost empty. The school holidays had not yet commenced, so we shared this wonderful stretch of sand with a scattering of other happy dog-owners. William by this time had attached himself to Judy, who was not a dog-lover, just a tortoise-fancier. As she ran along the beach, Wills looked up adoringly, while he kept in perfect step with each stride. However, when Kate started running in an attempt to exercise Wills, he performed an abrupt cartwheel directly underneath her feet sending her almost somersaulting into next week.

On arriving back home, I wore my 'I kiss better than I cook' apron to identify the exact standard of my culinary art, so we lived on barbecued fillet steak, or smoked salmon and prawns, or ham and sausages, plus a selection of mouth-watering salads and home-grown garden-minted new Charlotte potatoes (I grew the mint, not the potatoes!). My idea was to provide wonderful food without slaving over a sizzling stove. The cool white wine flowed abundantly throughout their stay, so no-one noticed that they were living entirely on salads! Judy kindly took us out to the Chichester Arms for supper on the night that Andy Murray was resting (we had cancelled our booking without compunction the previous night in order to watch the completion of his finger-biting match).

The day after Kate and Judy left, my lovely school-friend Jenny was due to arrive for the weekend. Some months before, I had telephoned her on the day before she was leaving for Antarctica. Having just lost my tennis-friend, also called Jenny, following a fatal brain bleed, when she was on the boat from Georgia, I felt like saying: "Please don't go." However, I knew I was being irrational, so I stayed tactfully tacit and wished her a tremendous, penguin-filled, trip. Unfortunately, Jenny was suffering from a severe cold and unable to make it down to Devon on this occasion, so I missed hearing all about her magnificent trip and seeing the spectacular scenes of this snowy continent. Jenny is very fond of Wills, so he reacted to this news by sulking all weekend.

I settled down to watching Murray putting up a brave fight in the semi-finals and narrowly missing a place in the 2009 finals. I felt for this young Scot, who, after so much hype in the press, had failed to realise his (and the rest of the country's) dream. When I watched Federer narrowly beat Roddick (16-14 in the fifth set after a gruelling 4 hours 16 minutes) to enter the history books as the greatest tennis player ever, I felt that Murray would have given the champion a good run for his money.

The next potential 'champion-of-all-time' arrived in the Barn for a holiday with her proud owners, Stuart and Laura. She was the cutest, smoothest three-month-old Labrador puppy that it was possible to meet, and although she was named Holly, there was not a prickle in sight. And she was not the colour of her namesake bush, but the colour of mouth-watering, good quality chocolate. On the top of her head, there was a cute bald spot; the result of an argument with a flower pot that had sharply won. William loved her. She was about a tenth of his mammoth size and enjoyed rolling beside him, round him and even under him in an effort to lie on her back in full and frank submission. She was taunting and tempting William's manhood, but when he became a little too frisky, she simply took refuge by slipping neatly under the car. She was due to start socialisation classes, which she clearly did not need, as she was already the most sociable puppy in the world.

When Stuart and Laura left a day early (Stuart's glider lesson had been cancelled due to the gale-like weather), I missed hearing the wonderfully pure sounds that had emanated from the barn, when this talented Royal Academy of Music graduate was practising playing his cornet. Normally, this hamlet is so quiet that you can hear the mice smiling: there is no roar of traffic, few cars, and the only sounds that we hear are those produced by cud-chewing cows, sheep giving birth, and sad little lost lambs, intermittently drowned out by the one-and-only barking mad dog! The barn and surrounding valley, that had come alive to the sound of music, became devoid of the uplifting melody and settled down to its usual rural murmurings, punctuated by the odd startled bark. Meanwhile, William looked everywhere for Holly; at the barn door, in the hydrangea bed, behind the lavender tubs and even under the car. His playmate, together with the classical music, had sadly evaporated into thin air.

CHAPTER 9

TREASURES IN THE ATTIC

After our last visit to France, Nick had left the boot protectors for his VW Golf and Mercedes in my attic. When Martin and family popped in for crumpets and chocolate cake rather earlier than expected (at lunchtime!), I asked him if he would kindly get the covers down for me. He willingly ascended the new staircase-loft-ladder and quickly became immersed in his collection of Watford Football Club programmes, believing that he could sell them on Ebay for a welcome profit. Maggie and Charlie shinned up the ladder with alarming speed, which reminded me of the times when I was about their age (and brave beyond belief) and I was invited to climb a long ladder and tumble into an open upper floor window for the 'finger-wiggling' neighbour, who had locked herself out of her house. When I ran downstairs and opened the front door, I was greeted as a heroine, out of all proportions to the task performed, but being the youngest of three children, I relished this rare opportunity to feel important.

The grandchildren enjoyed rummaging through the treasures in my loft-space, rather in the same way that my sister, Joyce, and I enjoyed playing with an enormous Victorian dolls' house that our grandfather had made for our mother, and which was kept in our grandparents' large attic in Bramhall. It was eventually donated to a wonderful orphanage in Barnet called Winifred House. Another story on this subject concerned one of my friends, who was busy making a dolls' house as a surprise Christmas present for his daughter, when she popped into the garage unexpectedly and caught him at work.

"What are you doing?" she asked.

"I am making a chest-of-drawers," he cleverly replied, to which she responded with innocent insight beyond her years:

"If you don't want to use it as a chest-of-drawers, it would make a lovely doll's house"!

There were no purpose-built homes for dolls in my attic, not even a bungalow or a flat (and fortunately, no mice at home), just boxes of Claire and Martin's treasures that had been left with me for safe-keeping when they had left home. Charlie found her father's toy 2CV car and Maggie found a red velvet jewellery box, which she generously gave to her mother. Martin kindly threw down the boot covers, before returning to rummage through a selection of items that had been long forgotten; an activity which was punctuated by his delightful and, at times, comical shrieks of unrestrained, unreserved nostalgia. The children were so excited to see their father happily lost in his childhood memories, that it prompted Maggie to inquire: "Daddy, did you have your bed up here when you were a boy?"

Two weeks before I was due to visit Ireland, Nick moved into his designer home. It had taken three years to renovate to the required high standard and, even more surprising, it was a staggering nine years since we had found it and dreamed of the glorious home that it would become. There were many hiccups on the way (that would take another 10 books) but amazingly, after this interminably slow (at times, halting) process, it was ready for occupation. I was very much looking forward to visiting Nick in his new home.

Before that, I had another knee-wobbling moment – I was informed that *William: Still Barking* had been published a month early. When the books arrived, I was very disappointed to find that the printer's palette had been too liberal with the pot of red paint. On the cover, I looked as if either I had fallen asleep in the sunshine, or was flushed with pride, or worse still, blushing from embarrassment! Dear reader, if you wear sunglasses, it does take the glow away and makes my skin appear less fiery. When Nick telephoned, I reported that I was unhappy with my scarlet face.

He replied: "Does William look all right?"

"He looks as gorgeous as ever," I said.

"That's fine then," he replied!

I sent a copy to my cousin, Claire, who had kindly edited the book for me (and who knows that we do not have lobsters in our family) and another to Allison in Australia for sending me the photographs of William to use in the book. Also, I gave a signed copy to John and Louise, and added: "With thanks for being such good neighbours."

I experienced an after-wobble, when, on the same day, I had an email from Halsgrove inviting me to appear at a number of book-signings, as these events are fine if there is a queue of people, but quite frustrating if no-one shows any interest. Reluctantly, I telephoned the stores to make the appointments. Then I spent an enormous amount of time sending blind email copies of a glowing résumé of the book to the hundreds of friends and colleagues on my email list and waited for the massive surge in sales! The Postmaster General became extremely irate and angrily returned masses of them, mainly because many overworked recipients had filled their mail boxes to overflowing and beyond. I also found out who was on holiday and whose address was redundant, so it was a neat way of cleaning up my address book.

The next day, I was delighted to enter a bookshop in Barnstaple and to see, in front of me, a copy of my new book proudly displayed on a pedestal in the centre of the shop. I was instantly recognised and asked to sign the copies that they had purchased. Not content with this limited amount of exposure, I dropped a copy of *William: Still Barking* into the *North Devon Journal* for review. Later, when I played tennis with the senior group at the indoor Tarka Tennis club, I took flyers down, and they all agreed that William was my twin!

My 'twin' and I linked up with some real twins. My good friend Claire came down to stay in the Barn accompanied by her son Angus, aged 13 years (now taller than me), and twin daughters Poppy and Sophie, aged 11 years. The twins are identical in every way, so much so that Poppy always wears something pink, as a way of distinguishing herself from her sister. This year, I was able to identify them more by personality. Poppy was more reserved, whereas Sophie (my god-daughter) was more of a drama queen.

Our party ventured with William to Saunton Sands, where the girls braved the icy water to go swimming. William stayed timidly at the water's edge until he saw a Springer Spaniel jumping nimbly over the waves. It was a beautiful, balletic sight. He then copied this method to reach the girls until the water became too deep, when he went swimming for the first time. A brave new world opened up for him. He spied a black Labrador, who was being thrown a large stick, much further than I could ever throw, into the distant rolling waves. William chased the male Lab (not the stick) using his newly-discovered dog-paddle, which was eminently effective – possibly due to his gigantic feet (good swimmers have large appendages). I understand that back-crawl takes a little longer to master, but now he can float, he is up for it. When his fur dried, it became not only a lighter shade of pale, but impossibly short and curly.

The children arrived back home with a generous present for William. It was the largest bone that William had ever seen. I think it either came from, or was destined for, the local lion house. He immediately became over-possessive, and whisked it away down the garden before any interlopers had the impudence to steal it from him. While we were having dinner, William arrived in the kitchen to settle down and nibble his prize. At one time, Poppy stretched her arm out in William's direction, and he gave a low warning growl in case she intended to take away his treasured bone.

The next day, the children wanted to return to Saunton Sands, this time with a newly-purchased bright-blue body-board. The girls managed to flop onto the board to catch a few waves, before gently floating to the shore. William bounded into the water, content to jump over waves and swim, without showing any interest in the intricacies of surfing, unlike some of the more adventurous dogs, who become water-born stars. When the girls started to shiver, Angus and I went to buy some ice-creams to warm them up!

Mayhem erupted in the shape of one over-excited dog. William spied the ices, so the twins started to jig around holding their treats high above their heads. William stood on his hind legs in an attempt to reach the choc-ice lollies, causing Poppy to cleverly leap onto a boulder out of his way. Then, in an instant, the hound-from-hell towered over Sophie, grabbed her choc-ice, scratched her chest through her swimsuit and rushed away with his trophy. Sophie was upset and rightly so. It must have been a shock for her to be faced with a giant dog, much taller than her, and even worse to feel his claws on her chest. Fortunately, he did not pierce her skin.

Claire, Angus and I offered to give her our ice-creams, but she was inconsolable. As we travelled home, Sophie started to recover her zest for life and when we arrived home, she said to me with almost adult appreciation: "I am all right now. Thank you for your concern."

I learned another lesson that day. We should have had ice-creams at the outside table with William chained to the table leg, as we did, with much success, the previous day. This incident also re-emphasized the importance of controlling dogs when they are with excitable children. Looking back, it would have been better to have found a spot on the beach that was not so packed with holiday-makers. When Wills was returning from the sea, a disgruntled holiday-maker shouted at him just as he was lifting his leg to pee on their billowing wind-break. Unfortunately this did nothing to staunch the stream, so I offered an equivalent flow of apologies before dragging my errant animal away, leaving the beach to the not-so-happy campers.

Finally, Claire and her happy family returned home, having had a brilliant holiday. I think William will miss them more than they will miss him. He loves children, as they provide excitement both in and out of the water. In dog years, this boisterous animal is two-and a half years old, which equates to about eighteen human years of age, an age when he should have reached maturity and started to settle down, but there is no sign of this happening this side of a distant Christmas.

I told Nick about William's swim. While he was very impressed with the hound's water-skills, he was fearful for his new pond – not the pond-life (which was non-existent), but the pond itself. He was frightened that Wills would dive straight in and perforate his expensive pond-liner, causing the water to drain away down to the lake. I suggested having a hose ready to squirt him if he ventured too close to the edge. When he was a puppy, I aimed a jet of water directly onto Wills's nose, so now he has a hose-pipe phobia and has not sunk his deadly teeth into one again.

My water baby received more visitors later that day. My niece, Alison, and her husband, Nigel, arrived with their sons, Oliver aged 13 years, and Morgan aged 11 years. Claire's son, Angus had kindly written a list of various pursuits for the boys to enjoy. The list included: Go-Karting (fab), cycling along the Tarka trail (funky), swimming in the pool (a bit wet), body-boarding (for girls), and playing Pooh sticks down by the river. William became madly excited and only calmed down when my daughter, Claire, arrived from London a little later.

Dinner was a disaster. Wendy Craig from the TV programme *Butterflies* would have excelled in comparison. My cooking, which had been enjoyed the week before, would have ranked 0/10. The (oven-ready) chips, which had so pleased Angus and the twins, blackened while we were drinking a chilled bottle of Taittinger champagne. In the heady haze, the apple crumble was completely forgotten, then heated a tad too fiercely, so that it developed a black top over an uncooked apple base. To complete my culinary excellence, I served Alison some orange fruit tea from a split bag. They all roared with uncontrolled laughter, a little too uproariously to my mind, when I timidly produced my 'I kiss better than I cook' apron. Morgan sighed: 'It's going to be a long night.'

I can remember when Claire and Martin were still at school, I discovered one day that I had absent-mindedly over-cooked the pizzas. I nobly said: "I will have the burned one", to which Martin swiftly replied: "Mum, they are *all* black." The children took over the cooking from that day on (and even for ever more). Sometimes, it is clever, even a little cunning, to make culinary mistakes.

The next night, Nigel offered to cook.

Not wishing to admit defeat, I declined the kind offer and tried to redeem myself a shade by producing a scorch-free meal. Luck was on my side, well, a helping of good fortune, coupled with a copious amount of nervous oven-inspection. I produced mouth-watering fresh salmon, perfect jacket potatoes and minted petite pois for the adults, and M&S fish fingers, crunchy oven-chips, garden peas with unlimited tomato ketchup (good for the prostate) for the boys. Not a meal that Raymond Blanc would have entertained, but one that would have made Rick Stein mighty proud.

William was less fortunate, as, after dinner, there were too many empty plates with fewer left-overs than the previous evening. Needless to say, he wolfed down some salmon skins and potato jackets eagerly, and not so politely requested some more. I thought I would quit cooking whilst I was ahead, so the next night (after I had driven for two hours to the University of The West of England in Bristol to meet my PhD student, Christine, and her Head of Studies, Nicola, and then driven for two hours home), the holiday-makers took the children to Pizza Hut. The following night, just before I left for Ireland, Alison and Nigel kindly took us all to the Chichester Arms to enjoy a proper meal.

CHAPTER 10

WILLIAM GOES TO IRELAND

William and I left Devon at 8am to drive up the M5, M6 and M51 to Holyhead, stopping briefly at Stafford Services to purchase some M&S food for my supper and a chicken sandwich for 'guess who?' We arrived at Holyhead six hours later, having stopped off previously at Holywell by mistake! Fortunately no-one was within earshot to hear my far from holy comments. I booked into the Travelodge, placed my suitcase in the first floor room, then went back for William. I entered the lift, but he stayed firmly outside whilst the doors closed on the lead. Another unholy panic! Fortunately I was able to press the 'Doors open' button before the lift ascended and join my stubborn hound. We took the stairs. Once in the bedroom, I took great care to put my suitcase out of William's range, placed his water bowl down and spread his green fluffy mat on the floor. He became a little truculent. He refused to sit or lie down on his mat, preferring, by far, to roll on the royal blue carpet in the bedroom, leaving enough moulting mane to make a mattress. I took him to Penhros Coastal Park, which was bathed in sunshine, where I telephoned Nick to let him know we had reached Holyhead safely. Wills let off steam paddling in the sea before rolling in ecstasy on, in and under the sand, until he resembled a writhing sand sculpture.

William slept well in the hotel that night. I wondered if I would wake up to find him on the bed with me in the morning with his nose against mine, or even lying on top of me, but he was happily spread-eagled on the blue carpet in a haze of fur and a good helping of Penhros beach.

I took him outside to pee, where I met a man who said: "Oh, you've got a furry one!"

"Yes," I replied, before feeding his furriness and running

my bath.

Wills had never seen me in the bath before, so it was comical when he peered over the side to sit and stare. His curiosity was satisfied in a nanosecond; he clearly did not appreciate this voluptuous vision of loveliness, as he kept his distance until I was up and dressed.

I packed the car, in two journeys; first William and then my suitcase. I picked up as much fur as I could from the carpet before, rather guiltily, closing the door of the room behind me and handing back the key. I guess this is why there was an extra charge of £17 for having a pet in the room.

We boarded the ferry. William stayed in the car with a bowl of water, the windows open and the alarm disabled. I found my cabin and lay down for the three hour journey (I sail better horizontally!). Fortunately it was calm. We disembarked into Dublin Port on the very Friday night that heralded the start of the Irish holiday season, so I opted to leave Dublin via the M1 toll road and arrived at Nick's house two hours later by this indirect route. William bounded out of the car in his enthusiasm to greet Nick, so we took him straight down to the lake at the bottom of the garden. This walk covers about a mile and a half so William was happy to have his supper and rest in his new purpose-built kennel for the night.

William steered clear of Nick's new pond with its expensive liner. We yelled "Aa Aa!" whenever he ventured too close to it. He was much more interested in rolling in a muddy trench that had been left by the mechanical digger, before rolling in the pile of grey sand that had been discarded by the builder. Each day, we hosed him down with the new outside shower (hot and cold mix – no less) before popping him in his 5-star kennel. This kennel is so large that Wills was able to entertain both Nick and myself inside – in fact he was planning a party there.

As I had time during my holiday, I decided that I would like to clean William's teeth. They were looking rather brown from a build-up of tartar. I had felt rather guilty that I had ignored the advice from dog training classes to get puppies used to having their teeth brushed each evening, ever since William had almost amputated my finger as a puppy. We chatted to a vet, who wanted to de-scale them under anaesthetic (wise lass), but I did not want Wills to risk an anaesthetic. Later, I spoke to a dog trainer in a super new pet shop in Cavan, who totally understood the problem. She sold me a very long toothbrush (the longest in the shop) and some special toothpaste that would remove the plaque from his teeth while he slept. I tentatively started to lift up his upper jowls and brushed his teeth. He liked the taste of it and adored the attention. Gradually, I was able to reach his back teeth both inside and out. So I now had a mutt with gleaming teeth and a 'ring of confidence' instead of a far-from-beautiful, mucky brown smile.

As the days went by William became less obsequious and more truculent. He bounded over the field, shortly to become a wild flower meadow, like a Springer Spaniel on hot coals. The fluidity of his movement was a joy to behold. Every time he circled the field, he always arrived back in his kennel before us with a haughty "What kept you?" expression.

One fatal day, he saw cows close to the hedge of the neighbouring land. He started barking. We called, whistled and shouted. He chose to hear nothing save his own incessant barking. All the cows lined up at the fence to see who was making this demented noise. William raised his barks a few decibels and moved forwards through fear (or was it bravery?). Nick waded through the long grass to put this still barking hound on the lead and take him back to his kennel.

It is an offence to frighten livestock even if they are frightening you. We were well aware that William could have been shot by the next-door farmer. We were concerned that this incidence could happen again with dreadful consequences. It was a stark reminder of the need to be able to control one's pet. On this occasion, I had failed miserably.

William had experienced a taste of freedom both in the field and in the lake, so it was no surprise to find that he did not want to jump into Nick's car. We airlifted him in when we visited the Royal Canal, where he refused to get more than his paws wet. A nautical dog, called Belle, who was swimming widths of the canal, failed to tempt him in, although it was obvious that he had bonded with her on dry land. We lifted him into the boot when we visited Greystones, South of Bray, where he simply sat and watched two Goldies having a whale of a time in the sea. Then we visited Laytown beach, South of Drogheda, with its swathes of shells stretching across the shore, where he ran in and out of the sand pools, while we looked for the perfect shell.

Even though he loved these visits, he became more determined not to travel by car, so when he was lifted in, he would immediately and irritatingly jump out. He wanted to stay at home and run down to the lake. Each day we walked him down to the lake, sometimes twice a day. At first he was tentative about paddling, but as the time went on, the ripples smoothed out until William forgot his fear and rushed to the Lough. He jumped over a wall a yard high into the water, causing a pair of swans with their six silver cygnets to glide away safely out of sight. He fetched sticks tentatively at first, but as his confidence grew exponentially, he retrieved them from as far as we could throw them. Each time he brought the stick to the edge of the lake (not to us!), so that at the end of the fortnight, it looked as if a wooden boat had been badly shipwrecked on the shore-line.

The next day was scheduled for us to visit Nick's new acquisition in Sligo, so that Wills could run about on the beach and run free in the sand-dunes. As we led him towards the car, he dug his heels in and point blankly refused to move. Nick tugged the lead, I pushed his rear and nothing, but nothing would make him budge. He was rooted to the spot and no amount of cajoling, pushing or pulling would make him move a millimetre. We were no match against his mighty strength. He had been in Ireland so long that he had turned into Paddy McGinty's goat.

We abandoned our visit to Sligo and took the stubborn goat down to the lake to swim. When Nick released his lead, Wills started frolicking in and out of the long grass like a playful puppy, who had cleverly outwitted his owners. Each of us relaxed and enjoyed another round of stick-throwing for our defiant water-baby.

The two-week holiday flew by far too quickly. We had settled into a routine, where Nick nobly took William out of his kennel at 7am. We bathed lazily and breakfasted on fresh orange juice and croissants, before I fed William and we walked down to the Lough together. We fitted in a number of visits out during the day, before walking Wills down to his beloved lake again. In the evening, whilst Nick was cooking dinner, I fed William, cleaned his teeth and put him to bed. He had loved his time in Ireland. When it was time to leave, he point blank refused to jump into my laden car. We lifted him in.

Our long trip home started when we said a fond goodbye to Nick at 5pm and made our way down the M1 to Dublin Port. There, while waiting in the queue to board, I let William jump out of the car for a last pee on the sweet-smelling rubbish bin before boarding the boat. Miraculously, he jumped straight back in. The man in the car behind mine came up to me and said: "What an obedient dog." If only he had known what a fluke this was and that, in truth, I was taking William McGinty home.

We boarded at 8.30pm and I found my cabin at the back of the boat and lay down. When I awoke, my cabin had magically changed around, so that now I was overlooking the bow! It took forever to unload this vast boat and even longer to find the Travelodge at 12.05am on a dark, rainy night. There, I slept for four hours before rising still in the dark at 5am to commence my six-hour journey home, along the M51, down the M6 and M5 in order to beat the holiday traffic, which clogs the motorways every single Saturday in the summer. We stopped only once at a M&S service station to fill up with diesel, collect a newspaper and purchase some groceries and give Wills his obligatory chicken sandwich.

William was in his element when we eventually arrived in Devon. He leapt out of the car and rolled over and over in the drive in unadulterated ecstasy, before lying on his back to expose his manly equipment. He was home.

CHAPTER 11

A LESS-THAN-
SUCCESSFUL SIGNING

I hoped that William would slot into his usual routine once he arrived home. This was not the case. When I walked him down my lane, he refused to turn back at the end when I said: "Over." He stood firm and the horns started to re-grow. I was sure that he thought that, if we went a little further, we would reach a beautiful swan-filled lake – a veritable paradise for aquatic canines. We had a serious conversation about Nick, holidays, and Ireland and I promised him that we would return for Christmas, if he was a good dog and that included turning round NOW. I think he got the message, as from that day onwards he became much softer and more malleable – dare I say even obedient.

After I had opened the post and dealt with it, responded to all my telephone messages and replied to 72 waiting emails, I started back to my normal routine of playing indoor tennis alternating with seeing patients at my clinics in Barnstaple and Taunton. At the Nuffield Hospital, Taunton, there was an envelope waiting for me from a Canadian lawyer. My heart sank. I imagined that it would contain a letter concerning an unhappy patient who wanted to take me to court. This is something that every single medical professional dreads. Even though one gives the best possible duty of care to all patients with medical rectitude, there is always the possibility that someone might want to buck the system to make a quick buck. Happily, it was nothing of the kind. Instead, it was from a man who had loved my book and wanted to tell me about his eight-year-old Golden Retriever called Rex, who was the spitting image of William. He even sent me photographs of his lovely dog, who accompanied the barrister to work and sat happily, tail wagging, while his clients told him their tales of woe. I wrote back to the lawyer thanking him for his kind comments and for sending me photographs of his handsome Rex. I told him that William would have loved his twin, but failed to tell him that my lad was not up to sitting still during my clinics!

Even so, William had been invited to one event that would require impeccable behaviour. In preparation for this, he had his teeth cleaned by the tooth fairy (me), who also doubled up as his ear cleaner and coat coiffeur. He had been invited to attend WHSmith's for his first book signing for *William: Still Barking*. Last year, when we were there to sign *Barking Mad in Barnstaple*, I forgot my pen and William knocked all the birthday cards off the shelf with one swish of his tail. I hoped that he would be more subdued this year.

The morning of his stately appearance, I received an email from the talented freelance photographer, Tom Teegan, who said that he had seen the photograph that he had taken of William and me on a poster in WHSmith's promoting the book signing. This delightful man offered to take some more shots free of charge. I immediately replied that I would love some more photos for the next book and informed him that he was mentioned in glowing terms on page 41 of *William: Still Barking*.

The book signing did not go as well as planned. We sold only nine books. Most customers wanted to purchase *Barking Mad in Barnstaple* to read first. Smith's had only three crumpled copies of this left and each of these sold out in the first ten minutes. Shoppers wanted to buy both books together. The dog-lovers made a great fuss of Wills, particularly the children, who had dogs, or even kittens or hamsters, at home. Then, a black male Labrador had the audacity to wander into the shop. William, who was retained by a lead fixed firmly under my chair, barked loudly. Both dogs let rip. The books on the table were sent flying. The queue of people standing patiently at the check-out craned their necks round to see who was disrupting their tranquil Saturday morning shopping. Wills was not a happy bunny. He was a frustrated dog, having to work against his wishes, wanting, more than anything, to be free to frolic with the fun-loving Lab.

The star of the book was, on the whole, thrilled to be stroked, cosseted and patted by the customers. Unfortunately, he did bark loudly at two men who bent down to stroke him. One of the men nearly fell backwards in shocked indignation. I could see that William had taken a dislike to these men, in the same way that he had previously responded by growling at one of my unkempt delivery men. I held him fast until they left the shop. I guess dogs, like humans, have their likes and dislikes, but it was decidedly embarrassing for me. The colour of my face matched the book!

While I was feeling pretty miffed with my discriminating man-hater (or protector?), Martin, Jo, Maggie and Charlie bounced into the shop. Sharp-eyed Maggie had seen the poster of 'William and Gran Gran' in WHSmith's window while they were shopping in Barnstaple, so they bundled in to meet me. It was a lovely surprise to see them. A kind lady dog-lover asked one of the young lads behind the till if Wills could have some water. This lad brought Wills a sweet little jam-jar lid containing not more than half-a-lap of water. He must have had a *very* small dog at home! After it was explained that Wills needed a bucket-full of water, a 'Roses' tin was brought containing ample water for his needs. William drank the water voraciously with obvious gratitude, taking great care to empty as much as possible onto the carpeted floor. Having quenched his thirst, my pet indicated to me that book signing was not for the faint-hearted. After he had been tied up for two hours, I decided that Wills was becoming fractious and had worked long enough, so I left the store to take my reluctant book-promoter home. He was obviously too exhausted (or too important) to jump into the car, so I heaved him into the boot and gently shut the lid.

William was rewarded for his efforts. My next barn guests, Gill and daughters Grace and Lucy, arrived with the cutest, sleekest little black Labrador named Lola. All his Christmases came at once in the shape of this friendly femme fatale. Wills was going to be drooling all week. He was free to enjoy 'whatever Lola wants' and 'whatever Lola does'. William swiftly became acutely disappointed, as Lola did not play fair. She kept trying to bite William's throat (apparently, she always went for the jugular), so I kept Wills away from his new girlfriend for the rest of their stay, in order to keep both dogs alive.

Disappointingly, Lola went for the throat of one of the

resident animals, with deadly consequences. She killed the largest, bonniest bunny, leaving a widow to cope alone with four lively youngsters. I had successfully protected them all year from William by clapping my hands loudly before he was allowed to play in the garden, but now a sprightly visiting dog had exterminated the daddy-of-them-all. This season, I had enjoyed seeing this family of rabbits eating their way through my verdant lawn and had been overjoyed to see the babies playing together, preferring to turn circles every-which-way and back again, rather than feeding incessantly and getting fat. Even more sickeningly, a crow had pecked out one of the dead rabbit's eyes. I commiserated with the family and gave him a suitable and fitting funeral close to his home in the brambles.

My 16th century cottage used to be covered in brambles during the 50 years when it was uninhabited. Brambles, nettles and ivy enveloped the farmhouse and both the adjoining cattle byres and barn. This Devon longhouse was lovingly restored (hopefully for posterity) in 1993 by The North Devon Historic Society and a full and fascinating history was written. My neighbour, John, showed me ten photographs of my cottage before it had been restored, which a friend of his had taken. They showed a derelict stone and cob cottage with a rusty, red corrugated roof, windows boarded up or missing, worrying cracks in the cob, huge ancient oak beams, and a proud chimney that was large enough to have started life as a lime-kiln. The photographer wanted me to have a copy of them in exchange for a copy of *Still Barking*, as he had read and enjoyed *Barking Mad*! This seemed an eminently suitable arrangement to me, and typical of the old days, when no money changed hands. So, I set to work scanning the photos into Power Point on my computer and printing them onto photographic paper. Kodak would have been very proud of the result. (I was, of course, an expert, as for ten years I was the physiotherapist for Kodak in Hemel Hempstead, when colour processing was at its height, before digital imaging took over!)

I compared the old photographs with recent shots of my cottage in amazement. My cottage had been saved from being another ruin, so it was now up to me to look after it for the next generation. In the 11 years that I had enjoyed occupying this uniquely historic cottage, I had built a bespoke conservatory and added an 'en suite' bathroom. My daughter, Claire, had been the designer when we lovingly restored the large muddy barn, with a mostly-missing tin roof, into spectacular accommodation for holiday guests. Recently, I have restored a cobweb-strewn attic into my office at one end of the barn and further 'en suite' guest accommodation overlooking the garden at the other end.

Even though my property has increased exponentially, William is only allowed into the kitchen, mainly because he sheds pillows-full of fur on a daily basis. This suits him fine, as he has never been allowed anywhere else. He is 'King of the Kitchen', though it would be most helpful if he would participate in some essential domestic duties, such as some cooking and clearing up.

However, I did notice that the King was shrinking. Martin thought Wills had lost weight when he saw him in WHSmith's. I thought that he had moulted most of his coat in the muggy weather and just 'looked' slimmer. I decided to take 'his snake-hipped highness' down to the vet's to be weighed. Wills was hesitant about standing on the scales at first, but eventually, a few treats from Helen later, he complied. In December 2008, he weighed in at 35.2Kg and now, in August 2009, he weighed only 34.4Kg. To my horror, he had lost 0.80Kg in eight months. This was not just a loss of puppy-fat, but a cause for alarm. I decided to fight this in two ways: firstly, by giving him larger helpings of food and secondly, by giving him a worm tablet (his last one was eight months ago). I crushed this mammoth pill, costing £7.80p, into some raw egg and mixed it in a monarch-sized meal. I hoped he was on the road to recovery.

While he was eating, I noticed that William had a very swollen anus. I wondered if he could have picked up an infection from the algae when swimming in the Lough in Ireland. I reckoned that he had made the problem worse by sitting in the car for so long on the trip to and from Ireland and that this may have been the reason why he did not like travelling in the car. I was concerned that this was the cause of his loss of weight, so I looked up 'Anal problems' in *The Seven Ages of Your Dog*, my dog bible, by Jan Fennell. There, I discovered that dogs have anal sacs, which may become blocked, and in older dogs can sometimes become cancerous. She suggested that owners of male dogs could be taught by the vet how to express them.

The next morning, I telephoned the vet for an appointment and saw Joss, a female vet, who expressed William's anal scent glands. Wills was extraordinarily phlegmatic and tolerant while he underwent this unpleasant operation. He stood still stoically, raising his deep brown eyes up to mine until they misted over. The smell was dire. In no way was it attractive to humans, even if it serves to identify a dog's territory or beckon all the beautiful bitches in Barnstaple to his bedside. I paid £26.37p for a procedure that Wills would rather not have had, but which included some bitter apple lotion to spray round the affected area to prevent him from licking this delicate skin and increasing any anal soreness. I reported that I had never seen William clean his bottom, to which Joss replied: "Perhaps he cleans himself, when you are not looking!" I was to go back to see the vet in a month's time if the condition failed to improve. Dear Jan, I failed to ask Joss how to express William's anal sacs, as I did not fancy the task!

I chatted to my friend Glennis, who bred William, about the problem of anal glands. She said that she had never experienced problems with her dogs, because in a pack of dogs (she has eight!), they lick each other's bottoms. This left me wondering who was going to attend to William's rear end? I love William to bits and therefore had taken on the duties of teeth cleaning, bathing, brushing, and feeding my hound but, for some reason, I baulked at the thought of giving his posterior a little lick. Instead, I sprayed him with a tasty mist of apple-aroma.

CHAPTER 12

BULLOCKS AND
BURIED KEYS

The next guests in the barn arrived unannounced. They had booked the previous year and, somehow, I know not how, I had not written the booking into this year's diary. While they sat in the drive, with their baby asleep in the car, I cleaned up and changed the bed and made everything as beautiful as I could. Thank goodness, I was not out by the sea with William. I was acutely embarrassed (red-faced again), so by way of apology, I left them a complimentary bottle of Merlot, asking them, while they were sitting patiently in the car: "Would you like it now?"

I always ask my guests if they like dogs and usually receive a mixture of comments, from those that love them more than life itself, to those who are extremely terrified of everything on four legs with menacing teeth. In this instance, my unexpected visitors replied: "Yes, we do, but our daughter is toddling." I quite understood and kept my apple-scented-animal well away from them, in case Wills made the already tense situation any worse.

No sooner had I retreated into my cottage than there was a knock on my door; my guests had a plaintive query: "There are no lights in the kitchen area. Please could you tell us where the switches are?" After my guests had tried changing each of the light bulbs, I lifted up the trip switch and mercifully the lights were restored. Phew, another close shave. I was not doing too well.

I decided that I would prefer to rent the barn out permanently. This would save me from cleaning the barn every week, washing the laundry and making more mistakes with the barn diary! Also, fewer holiday-makers had booked this year, so considering the price of electricity and the exorbitant Council Tax, I was only just breaking even. I placed an advertisement on the North Devon District Hospital notice board, which within the week brought a telephone call from a secretary, named Flavia. She viewed the accommodation the following Saturday while I was doing the change-over for the next guests to arrive.

Flavia arrived with her Collie, named Jim. The big test was to see if William and Jim would play well together. I need not have worried as the two dogs went wild together, circling the garden, and us, until William gasped for water and collapsed on the kitchen floor. He had exercised more vigorously than usual! Flavia loved the barn and immediately wanted to move in. However, Michael, my friend who had rented the barn for two previous winters wanted to come back as a permanent let. On each occasion, he had left the barn beautifully clean and tidy. I liked the idea of having a man around, particularly during the winter, so I agreed to let him come back as soon as my Summer season was over.

Within the week, Michael timidly telephoned to announce that he had found a house to buy. He apologised fervently, as he would not require the barn. I was very disappointed, but recovered slightly when I received another telephone call from one of his friends, who was looking for accommodation for herself full-time and her Royal Marine boyfriend at weekends. She arrived with a beautiful Springer Spaniel puppy. I showed them the barn and the fenced-in garden. Then I brought William out to see if he would play well with the puppy. All was going smoothly until two things happened. Firstly, on hearing that the guy had been serving in Afghanistan, I asked him: "Do you have the right equipment?" He looked at his girlfriend, then down at his crotch and answered: "I haven't had any complaints!" Secondly, William sat on the tiny puppy until it disappeared from view and started humping for England. Unsurprisingly, they made a swift exit, while the puppy was still intact.

My next guests in the barn arrived in the middle of a dinner party that I was giving for Jennie and Sally, my sex therapist friends. I wore my "I kiss better than I cook" apron, so despite my house guests refusing my best wine, the evening turned out to be as hilarious as usual. Jennie and Sally were given a guided tour of the new facilities and were suitably impressed. William was confined to the boot of the car until everyone had settled down in the kitchen and was ready to receive 'his nibs'. I had spent the day busily cooking some cheese straws to accompany the asparagus tips (from distant Peru), chopping up six different vegetables for a veggie hot pot and making a bitter/sweet apple tart from a supply of apples that John, my neighbour, had kindly given me. Dear reader, you will be pleased to know that I did not use any of William's essence of apple, though it was tempting! As I chopped and pared, I considered that I was in danger of getting repetitive strain injury from this unaccustomed exertion. Also, it was the first time that I had used my dormant rolling pin in ten years!

I think I must have tried to impress my friends a little too much with my home-made culinary efforts, because when I triumphantly placed the tart and Cornish clotted cream on the table, Jennie, my vegetarian friend, said: "Grace, I am sorry, I don't eat apples." After my superhuman efforts, I was crestfallen until she added: "Grace, I'm only joking!" Only true friends can get away with that!

The next morning, I attended to the washing up while Barry, my gardener, was hard at work mowing the lawn, which due to the rainfall this summer was growing at the speed of a space-rocket and was coloured the greenest of green. I mentioned that I needed him to attend to another job, but had quite forgotten what job it was! Well, I had forgotten until William started circling the garden with a potted clematis in his jaws. Sally had kindly and thoughtfully brought me two plants the evening before. William was reminding me the only way he knew how, in the same way that he had reminded Ian to take his helmet surfing, when he raced round the garden with this trophy!

Having shown Barry the exact position to kindly plant both clematis plants, so that they could wrap up my barn with a wonderful array of colour, I took William out for a walk. Just outside my wooden gate there was a steaming, wet cow-pat, which indicated that one of the bullocks must have escaped again. I hosed down the mess, keeping a wary eye on the drive for live-stock intruders. We then went for a scary walk, all the while wishing that I had taken a cattle-prod for good measure, before going to Barnstaple Croquet, Bowling and Tennis Club (no less) to play in a 'Veterans Mixed Tennis

William on the naughty step.
(Photograph by Julia Makin)

William at Crow Point.
(Photograph by Julia Makin)

Left: William doing what he enjoys most. (Photograph by Kate Spencer)

Below: Judy with William at Saunton Sands. (Photograph by Kate Spencer)

Above: William makes a friend. (Photograph by Kate Spencer)

Ready to go to Ireland.

William finds a rabbit hole in the garden. (Photograph by Allison O'Donaghue)

William's brother, William.
(Photograph by Natalie Stone)

William's brother, Frankie.
(Photograph by Lesley Durrant)

Above: William's pond in Ireland.

Swimming in Lough Sheelin.

William, Grace and Daisy.
(Photograph by Dorothy Gluck)

Right: Dorothy with Oscar. (*Photograph by Linsey Gluck*)

Left: Friends at Barnstaple Hotel.

Back row: Claire, Judy, Kate Middle row: Ann, Sally, Lyn, Jane, Front row: Glennis, Liz, Mary, Kay

Below: 'Twins'. (*Photograph by Tom Teegan*)

Tournament'. My partner, Alan, and I fared better than expected to reach the finals, before we were well and truly thrashed. I told Alan about the proximity of a young bull to my property and my phobic fear of bulls. This conversation triggered a frightening memory for him. He was walking through a field of cows with his elderly dog, when the herd stampeded towards him. Sensibly, he let his dog off the lead. Amazingly, this protective dog stood his ground and barked incessantly until Alan escaped with his life.

I prefer to play tennis indoors at the Tarka Tennis Centre, out of the rain, wind and glaring sunshine. One time when I came back from my regular Seniors' session, I was met by Zoë, one of my barn guests looking quite distraught. I wondered what disaster could have occurred to this young couple or, for that matter, to my barn. Apparently, her boyfriend, Ian, had risen exceedingly early to surf (a fact which was noisily noted by William) and had buried his car keys in the sand dunes above Saunton Sands. After enthusiastically catching the right sort of waves and surfing to his heart's content, he returned to the dunes to retrieve his keys. Unfortunately, the adrenaline rush must have dissolved his memory, because he could not find them anywhere. Not anywhere! He made a grid and searched each square. As luck would have it, he found a willing guy with a metal detector, but still he had no joy. Five hours later, he abandoned the search. Ian was still on the beach in his wetsuit, now undressed to the waist as his clothes, along with his mobile telephone and wallet were in his Mini.

Zoë was unable to hire a car, so she asked me with some desperation: "What should we do?" I drove Zoë to Saunton Sands, picked up Ian, whose wetsuit was now dry, and brought them back to the barn. Rather sheepishly, Ian asked his long-suffering house-mate to post his spare set of keys to him by special delivery, so that they would be sure to arrive the next morning. It was a great relief to this delightful, if dizzy, couple when the keys arrived in the post at 10.30am.

My barn guests were not alone in their dizziness. I am sad to report that I came into that category too. When I was last in Ireland, Nick kindly gave me a pearl necklace, so I brought it home and cunningly secreted it in my home in a place where no master burglar would ever think of looking. Now, I have totally forgotten where I have hidden it!

While I am driving the car, I try to take my mind back to obscure hiding places, but so far have had no luck. I drove William to Springfield Kennels prior to travelling by train to the Royal College of Surgeons in London to deliver a lecture on the treatment of male incontinence. All the while I was hoping for a 'Eureka!' moment, but instead settled down to read *Dog Heroes* by Ben Holt. It was not as if I was going to a function that warranted pearls, more that I was dismayed with my failing memory. Would my memory get worse? Would it abandon me altogether?

Dog Heroes is a most illuminating book written, following much research, about the many, many dogs, who have shown great courage saving human lives. I found it to be fascinating. Some dogs in the book were highly trained to rescue people, while others just relied on raw instinct to help those in danger, even though they may have been total strangers. People survived due to the actions of a number of dogs, from a variety of breeds, who performed amazing rescues from raging rivers, stormy seas, smoke-filled buildings and deep avalanches. It left me wondering if William was in this exalted league; if he would protect me to the ends of the earth; if he would be up to it when the moment came. I had a feeling that he would, but I sincerely hoped that I would never have to put this theory to the test. So far, William has only retrieved some sticks from the Lough in Ireland. Would he be willing to drag a human being back to dry land?

When I returned from London, I dashed off to collect my hound. As usual, I asked the lovely Linda for a full report. She was full of praise for my obedient monster, who, apparently, had played with an energetic male Golden Retriever puppy, until he (William) was exhausted. However, when he reached the comfort of his pen, he was not too tired to rhythmically thrust his hips against his green fluffy rug and have the mother-of-all humps! He never stimulated himself at home, so why was he exhibiting this behaviour when he was out? Was it as a result of the post-exercise adrenaline surge or was it because there was a pretty bitch in close proximity? My rumpy-pumpy animal did not have the vocabulary to tell me, though I guess he was simply displaying the actions of a testosterone-charged male with no-one to mount.

CHAPTER 13

WILLIAM HAS HIS
OWN AGENDA

I bumped into my friend Hilary outside Tesco's, which was wonderful as we had not been in touch for some time. We agreed to walk our dogs at Fremington Quay and then have a light lunch afterwards. On the day arranged, I brushed William until he shone and set off to meet Hilary. She had brought along her beautiful Tshi Tzu, named Sam. He was coloured silver, had a central parting and wore his fur down to the ground like a long silky evening skirt, which swung seductively with every hip movement. He was a supreme example of his breed.

As we walked along the old railway track footpath, we let the dogs off their leads and were amazed how they avoided the many families of cyclists who owned the track. It was a splendid autumnal day, with the benefit of left-over summer warmth, which, coupled with such stunning scenery, made us feel fortunate to live in such a lovely area. We eulogised poetically about the raw beauty of the countryside in this particular corner of North Devon. This euphoria was short-lived, as things quickly started to deteriorate. William spied a muddy ditch; true to form, he wallowed in it until he was black. Only the top of his head and his blonde tail were spared. Hilary and I laughed at the difference between her pristine pooch compared with my mucky mutt. William was beyond help. I had hoped that my dog had grown from a mud-loving puppy into a responsible adult. But no, you can get the mud out of the dog, but you cannot get the dog out of the mud.

Things changed when we turned back and headed for home. Sam followed his larger friend everywhere in an attempt to be one of the pack. William dived into the bushes, swiftly followed by Sam, who completely disappeared from view. When this eclectic pack emerged, Sam looked as if he had been drowned in an oil sump; he was blacker than a coal-face worker. Every inch of his fur, from his nose to his toes, was the colour of charcoal; only his eyes were spared. Hilary and I laughed hysterically until our faces hurt; even the track-loving cyclists giggled as they wobbled past.

When we reached the car park, William point blank refused to jump into the car. I placed a bowl of water in the boot, but my grubby muffin determinedly stood his ground. I sighed while I lifted my highly-smelling hound into the car, opened the windows, disabled the alarm, then rushed off to scrub my hands clean before enjoying relaxing over a delicious lunch. Hilary and I agreed that next time, we would take the dogs to the beach. Sand was preferable to mud. When I arrived home, my guests, who were honeymooning in the barn, must have seen William through rose-coloured spectacles, as they thought that he was wonderful just as he was – a friendly, filthy, feisty dog with bags of character. I was not so sure, so I hosed every crusty corner of his grubbiness, letting the oil slick deluge down the drive, until he was nearly as clean as a whistle and infinitely more acceptable. Later, I cleaned the evil-smelling hatch-back boot until it sparkled again.

William was sweet-smelling when I left him at Springfield Kennels for another mini break. I opened the car and he ran into the field at the speed of a quick-fire laser, without looking back or even wishing me a good time. I met Nick in Westonbirt Arboretum for lunch before travelling to Burford for a reunion of the 1959 physiotherapy set from the Royal London Hospital School of Physiotherapy. To celebrate being 'Friends for 50 Years' we dined, with partners, in a beautiful private room at The Bay Tree hotel. It was a hilarious evening with so many happy (young) faces, who all enjoyed this special and unique celebration. Our habit of making the men move round the table after each course confused the hell out of the waitresses, who found our fun and frivolity to be infectious. Most of us stayed the night, so met at 9am the next morning for breakfast, to continue the jollity and catch up on everyone's news. All of us deemed the evening to have been a great success and eagerly promised to meet again, at the same venue, next year.

Nick and I stayed in the Costwolds for the rest of the weekend and were able to visit the picturesque villages of Broadway and Bourton-in-the-Water, where the beautiful soft yellow sandstone cottages glowed in the autumn sunshine, which cast low shadows over a profusion of 'olde worlde' scenes, creating a paradisaic panoply for the artists' palette.

After such a brilliant weekend, I drove to the kennels to collect young Wills. John gave me an excellent report – no misdemeanours – my puppy had grown up into a fine adult dog, who was becoming a bit boring! Wow, I had dreamed of the day when he would settle down, but now that he evidently had, I felt wistful for the unique, unpredictable muffin that had previously caused so much mayhem and amusement.

William did not sit on his laurels for long. While Barry, my gardener, was busy cutting the grass, my hound was just as busy emptying the contents of a flower pot all over the drive. I replanted the newly-potted plant and prayed that it would live a long and healthy life, despite its upheaval, before sweeping up the many scattered clumps of leaf-mould. Afterwards, I went up to my office to make the telephone calls that I had promised Nick I would make on his behalf.

CHAPTER 14

MORE PUPPIES!

In Ireland, Nick was busy getting his house in order, an activity that meant placing bright coloured stickers – in often inaccessible places - wherever there was a snag needing attention. Many stickers later, he asked if I would help him. He wanted two Flatcoat Retrievers as pets; not puppies, but one-year-old dogs who had been already trained. He had obviously come to this conclusion after reading *Barking Mad in Barnstaple* and wished to avoid the puppy stage! I volunteered to help him in his search for the perfect pet, if there was such a thing. These dogs had to have good bladders, come immediately when called, walk to heel, and retrieve beautifully. They were not destined to be gun dogs, but were to be great company for Nick.

I telephoned The Flatcoat Retriever Society of Ireland, the Irish Flatcoat Retriever Society, and the Flatcoat Retriever Co-ordinator in England to find that these much-in-demand breeds were in short supply. In Edinburgh, there was a possibility of puppies in the Spring (in six months time), but that seemed to be too long to wait. I was warned against having two puppies of the same age, because if one died, there was a chance that the other one would keel over, too. I was advised to stagger the dogs' ages. I discovered that very few breeders sold trained dogs. I was told that I would miss out on the fun and frivolity of the puppy stage!

The receptionist at my local Vet gave me the telephone number of her sister and brother-in-law, who were considering having a Flatcoat Retriever litter, when their bitch was in season. This lovely couple, Chris and Julia, train gun dogs and are themselves judges in this field. I was invited to their farm, close to Instow, to meet their (hopefully willing) bitch and witness a competition on the last night of a weekly training course that they had been running from April to September (with time out for hay-making). The prospective father, Tudor, was there, as he was one of the dogs being judged. I was most impressed with the heel-walking and retrieving of these newly trained dogs and vowed to enrol William into next year's course.

Chris agreed to let me know when the puppies were to be expected and to reserve two male puppies for Nick. Both of us would visit them during their training period. I was told that a new puppy would cost £650 and a fully trained dog would cost £1300. We waited eagerly for news.

While I was waiting, William and I appeared at Trelawney Garden Centre, Ashford, for a book signing of *William: Still Barking*. We sold none of these books, but sold six copies of *Barking Mad in Barnstaple*! William was good promotional material and surprisingly well-behaved. No tantrums, no barking and no general running amok. After two hours, we called it a day, whilst we were ahead, and headed for home. Claire and her white lop-eared rabbit, Pablo (mark II) were coming for my birthday weekend, so I needed to shop and prepare for their arrival. (Pablo mark I ran free in a flat in Amsterdam – when Claire wanted to stay a little longer over Christmas, she asked her neighbour to post some more carrots through the letterbox!). Claire was partial to fish and vegetables; whilst her new rabbit preferred grass garnished with dandelions. William swiftly volunteered to look after young Pablo, who sounded tasty beyond belief.

It was difficult to keep William confined to the kitchen, when there were rabbit smells emanating from the guest bathroom. Thoughtfully, young Pab always left his waste pellets deep inside his cage, even though he was free to roam over my new white tiles. Claire barricaded the wire to the heated towel rail to avoid a gnawing disaster. Somehow, this gorgeous rabbit survived his holiday, though it could have easily had a different outcome. I bought Pablo a bright red rabbit harness (a bargain at £3), so that Claire could walk him on the lawn. She togged him out resplendently in the conservatory and held firmly onto the long lead. Within minutes, this young furry creature had hopped right out of his harness in a bid for freedom. He became a demented white puff-ball, twisting and turning in the manner of an Olympic high-jumper with attitude. I shudder to think what would have happened if he had escaped from my lawn. He almost certainly would have joined the wild rabbits in the brambles, but would have lacked the wily cunning to survive in the wild. His trademark, whitest-of-white albino coat would have been clearly visible to every small-animal predator.

The day after Claire and Pablo II left, my school-friend, Jenny, arrived from Hatfield Heath. After her long journey, William gave her a rousing welcome by wagging his tail in circles in an effort to whip up enough power to launch his vertical jumping routine at the kitchen window. We took him to Crow Point, where he behaved himself impeccably. That is to say, he kept clean, returned when called, and jumped back neatly into the car. There was no humping, no ploughing through mud and, thankfully, no humping anyone in the mud. Jenny was impressed. He had grown up. She had thoroughly enjoyed *Barking Mad*, so I gave her a copy of *William: Still Barking*.

After Jenny left, I rushed down to St John's Garden Centre for another book-signing. I was given an office chair, complete with castors, to sit on. I needed to anchor Wills's lead to my chair, to prevent him from wandering off. As I asked one of the lads for a more stable chair without wheels, I had visions of my not-so-trusty steed leading me at full pelt through the Garden Centre, with his ears flapping wildly and with me trailing behind him, crying plaintively for him to stop, like a chariot race to the death!

Once anchored, Ben Hur's steed was great with the children (even though some had their faces painted as terrifying tigers, and some as flighty butterflies) and adults (unpainted) for an hour-and-a-half, but when a rather unsavoury man crowded him, he leapt forward and barked. I decided to leave before there were any complaints. I had signed six copies and had a chat to one lovely lady who brought her shooting-seat, so that she could sit next to me while she asked me to sign her own copies of both books. She had read my first book twice whilst on holiday and was currently enjoying the second. As she lived locally, she was desperately trying to work out, from the literature, where I lived. I was delighted, nay overjoyed, that the accounts of William's shenanigans had given her so much pleasure.

It was not just William who was up to no good. I took him out in the dark for his last walk of the evening and noticed a man leaping over my neighbour's wall into the lane. John has spikes on his farm gate and keeps it locked at night, but this guy was vaulting quite nimbly over the adjoining wall. William started barking loudly and straining at the lead. Rather than being pulled into an unwanted somersault down my acutely steep drive, I let him go. I imagined he would frighten, or even bite, the intruder, but all he did was lick him all over!

"Can I help you?" I asked boldly.

"Is John in?" the young man asked. "I owe him £50."

I asked him to leave it in the letterbox and telephoned John the next morning. He knew the guy, so all was well. This scenario showed me that William was no good at arresting criminals. I was on my own!

I had to take my felon-licking dog to Springfield Kennels, as I was scheduled to travel to Liverpool to deliver a repeat of my Professorial Lecture at the Chartered Society of Physiotherapy Annual Congress. I elected to travel by car for convenience, but my gardener, Barry, told me that the M5 motorway was jammed South of Bristol due to an unfortunate incident. A lorry had hit an electric pole, causing the electric cables to fall across both carriageways. I set off, making sure to listen to the travel report on the radio, and heard that the M5 would be shut in both directions all day. My head hurt. How could I bypass this section of motorway? By the time I had reached Tiverton, my mind was made up; I would travel by train. Twenty minutes later, my headache evaporated and I was standing on a very packed train hunting for a spare seat and was lucky to find one. I changed at Birmingham with one minute to catch the Liverpool train. It is amazing how it is possible to sprint while carrying an overnight bag, if one is sufficiently challenged. I jumped into this connection just as the doors slid shut.

The next day following my presentation titled *'Under Every Good Man....'*, I left Liverpool for my return journey. Six hours later, I arrived at Tiverton Parkway station more than ready for a pee, only to find that the station was firmly closed. I muttered a mild expletive, which aptly described my predicament; unfortunately, this was overheard by two young lads sitting on the station bench.

"The stationmaster went home early, as he wasn't feeling well," one of them reported, while the other chipped in: "You'll have to find a bush."

I noticed that there was no-one in the car park, so I squatted down beside my car as directed and, with as much dignity as I could muster, I emptied the entire contents of my bladder causing a veritable flood over the station yard. The relief was instantaneous and my glazed expression probably matched William's, when he answers a call to nature. Why is it that we encourage animals to perform in the open, but humans are discouraged from a similar activity? It seems a little unfair. I was merely helping to redress the balance.

When I collected my hound from Springfield, John told me that he (Wills not John) had been eating his blue plastic bed. I was sorry to hear that he had reverted back to his former destructive puppy ways, when he chewed through much swish plastic bedroom furniture until he was destined to sleep on a flat, furry green mat.

The next day, Christine, one of my PhD students, arrived with her supervisor, Nicola, for a tutorial. Nicola brought a delicious home-made chocolate chip cake, which we enjoyed for tea. I kept 'his nibs' in the kitchen while we had our meeting followed by a light lunch in the conservatory. Christine had, kindly and thoughtfully, given William a bone, so while we were meeting, I let him take it into the garden. He was more interested in talking to my visitors than chewing as planned. He kept looking in through the large glass windows and danced a jig every time they looked at him. He could have been on the stage. He threw his bone up into the air and rolled gleefully over it, making sure he had gained my visitors' full attention. He certainly knew how to work the room. This 'remember me' programme was completed by a feverish finale of incessant barking until he was invited inside.

I kept Wills in the kitchen when a prospective tenant came to view the barn for a long-term let. I had found letting my barn for the holiday period meant that every Saturday during the season, I was confined to cleaning the barn, changing the beds and washing all the laundry ready for the next holiday-makers. I was fed up with my repetitive cleaning duties. A long-term lodger was the answer. Clive arrived in a smart Mercedes, but surprisingly stayed in his car in the drive until I greeted him. He was frightened of the wild dog at the window of my kitchen who was heralding his arrival. He felt that this animal might jump up. I left my jack-in-the-box in the house and swiftly invited Clive into the barn. He loved the feeling of spaciousness, with the high vaulted ceiling and mezzanine bedroom, and immediately wanted to live there. He signed the six-month contract and gave me the first month's rental in preparation for moving in, in one month's time. I hoped that he would make friends with William, as Wills would certainly like a new play-mate. William had one month to learn not to jump up!

CHAPTER 15

TALKING DOG FOR SALE

Glennis invited me to her home to see her new puppies before they were re-homed. I was met by Frankie, William's brother trying to leap over the child-gate towards me. Glennis had eight adult dogs in her kitchen, so I had to identify each one by name and give each of them a special nuzzle. Frankie, the supreme dog, was my clear favourite. This champion dog had put on some weight since I had last seen him, so he was not looking as svelte and snake-hipped as his brother, Wills, but then I was impossibly biased! There were two female and two male puppies, about the same size and shape as William was when he first came to live with me. They were born from the same parents, so they were, in fact, brothers and sisters to Wills and Frankie. Glennis asked me if I would sign some *Barking Mad* books so that she could give each of the puppy purchasers a signed copy of the book, as it included their family tree. We both laughed knowingly when Glennis said: "If they had read this book before collection, they would have turned tail and run!" I cuddled both the male puppies. They were adorable. I had forgotten how small and silky my lad had been when I collected him. I knew that I would never rear another puppy, but I fell in love with both these cute little guys, so I was very glad that they were promised to other families. Incredibly, both boys were going to be called Oscar.

When I lived in Chesham Bois, I had a glorious white Persian cat, bred from supreme champions, whom I named Oscar. On one occasion, when I took him to the vet, the nurse called out: "Oscar!" Three people in the waiting room stood up and made for the door. There were two dogs similarly named, as well as my handsome puss. I had to wait my turn until Oscar Dorey (cat) was duly called.

As I was going through a serious 'puppy-mad phase', I

75

telephoned Julia to see if her flat-coat bitch was in season. She let me know that her female dog was not yet calling for a mate, but as the year was coming to a close, she may well be mated next Spring, when puppy rearing would become easier. I was disappointed, as I was looking forward to watching Nick's two puppies being put through their paces. It seemed an interminably long wait.

I decided to convey the 'puppy-delay-news' to Nick in person, when I visited Ireland two days later. I left William at Towsers Kennels and jumped on a plane from Exeter Airport. I travelled with only hand-baggage, as Nick had stocked my side of the wardrobe with toiletries for me, and as I had a warm jacket and boots there, I could travel light. Nick collected me from Dublin Airport, which was such an easy journey in comparison to the long trip to Holyhead, when I took William over in the Summer. But almost immediately, I missed having him there with me. Nick felt the same.

We walked down to the lake with Jim and Margaret, friends visiting from Bushey, Hertfordshire but even with their great company, I missed my rascal. I peered over the lakeside wall, to see if the sticks that my water-hound had lovingly retrieved were still there. I saw only one solitary stick floating aimlessly at the edge of the Lough; the others must have simply been swept away. I looked across the Lough and imagined my hound swimming way out, in an effort to breathe and retrieve at the same time. The kennel looked empty and lifeless, though I noticed that there was now a new mounting block so that William could reach the upper level. I wondered if he would still be wary of the top bunk or if he would still choose to sleep on the floor. This visit, of just under a week, went far too quickly, but I had to be back for my patients who were booked at the Nuffield Hospital, Taunton.

Maddeningly, only one patient was booked for my clinic the next morning and she failed to appear, as she had not received her appointment because of the postal strike. I had travelled for an hour to Taunton, waited hopefully for half an hour, and spent another hour driving home. I could have stayed with Nick for longer. I seem to have two lives: one wrapped round my professional life, advising men and women with incontinence and sexual dysfunction, training nurses and physiotherapists, writing books and articles, and supervising

PhD students; and one that is pure pleasure with Nick.

While I was airborne, I read *Dewey* by Vicky Myron, a delightful and often heart-rending book about a tiny ginger kitten, who was dropped into the night drop box of the library in Spencer, Iowa, on the coldest night of the year. He was found in the morning, frozen, grubby and hungry by Vicky Myron, the dedicated library director, who attended to his frost-bitten paws and nursed him back to health. Dewey took up residence in the library and quickly became a celebrity, not just in the locality, as his fame spread to reach the world-wide stage. His story was so poignant and well-written that I found myself falling in love with him too.

When I collected Wills from Towsers, I was informed that he had found a new love in his life, a fair two-year-old Labradoodle named Willow. William and Willow; they sounded well together. W&W. It was not just their names that blended together; they fused together at playtime, romped round the field in unison and became bosom friends. I expect they would have loved to culminate their romance by producing some raw Retrieverlabradoodles!

Despite leaving Willow, William enjoyed his homecoming. He rolled in the drive, visited the garden, lapped his water bowl dry, before settling down to claim his kitchen. The next day, the builder and joiner came round to estimate the cost of producing a new bespoke kitchen and oak staircase. This upheaval would take two months (minimum?). Unfortunately, I could not move into the barn, as my lodger had signed a six-month contract. Wills would have to move into the conservatory along with the china, pots, pans and microwave – unless he stayed in Ireland with Nick??? Could I cope with life without my two best friends? The answer was a resounding 'no', but if things became too tricky, it was always an option.

I mulled over the possible options and went to play indoor tennis. Ches arrived at the same time as I did (always early) and, knowing my love of dogs, gave me an email that he had been sent. I have decided to share it with you. It read:

A guy is driving around the back woods of Montana and he sees a sign in front of a broken down shanty-style house: 'Talking Dog For Sale'. He rings the bell and the owner appears and tells him the dog is in the backyard. The guy goes into the backyard and sees a nice looking Labrador Retriever sitting there. "You talk?" he asks. "Yep.' the Lab replies. After the guy recovers from the shock of hearing a dog talk, he says: "So, what's your story?". The Lab looks up and says: "Well, I discovered that I could talk when I was pretty young. I wanted to help the government, so I told the CIA. In no time at all, they had me jetting from country to country, sitting in rooms with spies and world leaders, because no-one figured a dog could be eavesdropping. I was one of the most valuable spies for eight years running. But the jetting around really tired me out, and I knew I wasn't getting any younger, so I decided to settle down. I signed up for a job at the airport to do some undercover security, wandering near suspicious characters and listening in. I uncovered some incredible dealings and was awarded a batch of medals. I got married, had a mass of puppies and now I'm just retired.". The guy is amazed. He goes back in and asks the owner, what he wants for the dog. "Ten dollars." the guy says. "Ten dollars? This is amazing! Why on earth are you selling him so cheap?". "Because he's a liar. He never did any of that."

This made me consider the vocal mutterings of my own dear beast. He produces a range of noises designed to suit a number of disparate occasions, commencing with a low-pitched whine, when he is left for more than four hours, rising to a series of loud and excited woofs to announce the arrival of visitors, reaching a crescendo of eardrum-splitting barks, if he is startled at night. Other than that, he is the proverbial much-loved dumb animal. Most of the time, when we are happily together, at home, out walking, or in the car, he is as mute as a dumb-bell – just as heavy and twice as beautiful. However, to casual visitors, when he is on protection duty, he becomes a barking-mad jack-in-the-box, with a threatening demeanour.

The South-West of England suffered from a severe storm with lashings of horizontal rain, which blew up my drive at a million miles an hour until it felt as if the roof was going to lift off my cottage and fly perilously into orbit. Claire was meant to be arriving from London for Martin's birthday, so I persuaded her not to set out in such inclement conditions. Her car would have been blown from lane to lane on the motorway, which was bad enough, in itself, without possible delays from severe flooding and the ghastly prospect of being struck by falling trees. Throughout the storm, William stayed tacit. There was no thunder and lightening, so nothing to trigger a round of fearful nocturnal barking. As I lay in my bed, totally unable to sleep, there was not even a whimper from my hound, though to be honest, I had pulled the duvet over my head until it was deep inside my eardrums.

It was no surprise, in this ugly weather, that no-one attended my book-signing at Waterstone's Bookshop. I sat patiently for an hour, this time without the star of the book, until I felt that I could use my time more effectively at home. I left early, leaving a pile of books duly signed, with the manager's adage ringing in my ears: "A signed book is a sold book." I admired his optimism. However, that evening when I fired up my computer, I received an email from Trelawney Garden Centre: "Please could William and I do another book-signing in the run up to Christmas?" I consulted his nibs. It was after all his third birthday. We agreed to give it a (final) shot.

CHAPTER 16

THE NEW KITCHEN

I decided to give my farmhouse kitchen a makeover. My kitchen, to date, consisted of a large room, with three impressive 500 year-old oak beams spanning its width. In one corner was a ghastly pine staircase, varnished orange, which led up to my bedroom and my beautiful new 'en suite' bathroom. Storage space consisted of awful pine cupboards, a rather fetching large nine-foot pine dresser, which I bought from the previous owners of the cottage, a mahogany chiffonier, which belonged to my maternal grandmother, a dark green ESSE cooking range underneath a large stone chimney, complete with bessemer beam, a tall refrigerator and a black oven. The oven was purchased after a woodlouse had the gall to fall from the old chimney into some soup on the stove, then the ESSE gave up the ghost, I think, more in protest than from an oil blockage that the plumber had long predicted. In the middle of the room stood a large antique pine table, delivered in a panic on Christmas Eve, and four pine chairs with fronds of raffia, cane, wicker, or what-you-will, descending from underneath the seats and left dangling by a young exuberant puppy named William.

The floor was covered with some poor-quality quarry tiles, which had served well in those puppy-leaking days; days that were only a 'never-to-be-repeated' distant memory. I purchased twenty-five square metres of old local delabole slates from my window cleaner as a starting point, on the understanding that I could have his cute little grey 'sound-muffler' dog, too. That was until the cutie barked repeatedly (a little dog with a big vocal cords), when the arrangement was quickly amended to contain only the slates. I received a quotation for a new staircase, made from seasoned oak, from a local joinery firm, and estimates from my reputable builder, electrician and plumber. I enjoyed several 'shopping' days visiting local industries, to source the best cooking range, fridge-freezer, Butler's sink, taps and seasoned oak table. I had to move fast as VAT was set to increase in 2010.

The kitchen designer failed to arrive, but instead sent a guy to measure up. After he left, I telephoned the kitchen designer and invited her over to view my unique kitchen to make sure that her vision was at one with mine.

The operation 'new kitchen' was due to begin in the middle of January. I had not warned my 'kitchen dog' that his 'home' was about to be dismantled, advertised in the local press, sold where possible, dumped, or made into firewood (not dear granny's dresser). I would make a temporary kitchen in my conservatory, where I would camp out with a table, chair, fridge, trusty microwave and little else! Wills would join me there.

I camped out with my pillow and duvet in the sitting room when Maggie and Charlie came for the night, to prevent them from meeting William in the kitchen on their way upstairs to find me in my bedroom. Maggie found a photograph of Nick and me on my 50th birthday, which he had kindly organised for all my friends years ago. I was wearing a black, designer, off-the-shoulder dress, which generated a puzzled question: "Was that photo a long time ago, because your shoulders are showing?"

"Yes, that was a lovely dress but I don't have it now," I replied, to which Maggie commented: "Did you grow out of it?"

We settled down to make surprise Christmas cards for Mummy and Daddy, so I encouraged the children to keep our clandestine activity a secret, and we agreed to send the cards to their parents by post. Then they made cards for each other, which Martin saw, when he came to collect the girls.

"How lovely, you've been busy making Christmas cards.", he said.

"No, Daddy," they said in unison. "We have not been making Christmas cards!"

After the children had gone home, I took Wills down the lane for a walk. All went well until I saw a schoolgirl riding a pony coming towards us. I did an about turn and led my excitable hound back up the hill towards my cottage. The pony changed gear to a canter and started gaining on us. I reached my steep drive just in time, thinking a potential incident had been avoided, until William turned and reared up on his hind legs making a dive down the drive towards the hapless pair. I had to use superhuman force to hold onto my powerful brute, who was using every tense muscle and sinew to resist me. I had flashes of a bucking pony throwing its rider, head first, onto the hard, unforgiving road. I held the lead tight and yelled "Aa Aa!" Immediately, Wills sat down, tail wagging and watched the startled rider continue her journey. With hindsight, I think my best friend was protecting me and my property by doing his utmost to prevent a large beast from clip-clopping up my drive. Once they had passed by, he was as happy as Larry.

I took my happy chappy to Colyford, near Seaton to visit Mary and Tony, who have been close friends since my Amersham days. The journey was a little treacherous with the low sun in my eyes, but infinitely better than the return journey, where I was trying to miss the puddles in the dark, with the windscreen wipers on full pelt. I arrived to a cloudless blue sky, with the sparkling sun shining its heart out. It lifted our spirits, as we walked Wills around their beautiful garden. Although I was expecting total havoc in the vegetable plot, Wills kept to the lawn and behaved impeccably. He was confined to the garden by a low fence, covered in wire mesh, which prevented the local rabbits from devouring all the healthy vegetables. Thankfully, even though we knew he could, he did not even attempt to jump over the low fence to reach the chickens and horses in their adjoining field. He deposited a large offering at the edge of the compost heap, in, apparently, the best spot possible, where he received hearty congratulations from Tony, quite out of all proportion to the job done.

The adjoining newly acquired field, called Mary's Meadow, was crying out for a donkey or two. Tony only wanted livestock he could bring to the table, while Mary fancied being a proud donkey owner. She told me about the Donkey Sanctuary at Sidmouth, where poorly donkeys are nursed back to health in spotless stables. Admission is free, but, very cleverly, donations are gratefully received. I made a mental note to take the grandchildren there, next time they stayed with me, as it would make a welcome change from the Gnome Reserve.

I began to think it was about time that I was put out to grass! After two or more years of frustration with the NHS, I suddenly decided that I had had enough. It was 47 years since I had started work at Harrow Hospital, as a full-time donkey for £10 per week. I had been at North Devon District Hospital for 11 years and, as a specialist physiotherapist, helped to set up the Continence Service in the Ladywell Unit. Now, my major complaint concerned follow-up appointments for existing patients. I have a duty of care to the patients that I treat, but new patients were being given appointments ahead of existing patients. When I see a patient, I may wish to see them again in 2, 4, or even 6 weeks. Instead, my patients were being sent appointments in 3 or 4 months' time. When I have asked for my existing patients to be given appointments ahead of new patients, I was told that the government targets have to be met. I shall continue to give the best service that I can to men and women privately at the Nuffield Hospital, Taunton and at Queen's Medical Centre in Barnstaple and, of course, I shall continue as a PhD supervisor and will lecture as requested.

Meanwhile, I was 'project-managing' an extensive kitchen refit, at the same time as trying to tame a mischievous dog. This lump of blessed willfulness decided to empty a bag of house coal, which I had left outside my sitting room door, so that I would not have to carry it far. I realized that my rule of 'leaving nothing outside' had sadly slid, when I was confronted with a black-faced dog sitting in a pile of coal, which covered, yes covered, my recently steam-cleaned drive. William was not even the slightest bit apologetic. The word 'contrite' was foreign to him. His demeanour resembled a grubby 'Just William', but with a wickedly whirling tail. I swear he was smiling when I led the sooty-nosed criminal inside and donned my faithful yellow rubber gloves to fill the brass coal bucket that my dear father had made.

William was now three years old or 21 years of age in human terms. He had celebrated his birthday at Trelawney Garden Centre, where he was needed for yet another book signing. Once there, he decided to party, even though he was restrained by his lead. He shuffled the books around on the table until I announced that the party was over and that the birthday boy should return home, where he continued his shuffling, this time with coal. He should by now have developed into a responsible well mannered adult, able to consider other members of the family. Instead, he was a mischievous, fun-loving, crazy beast. A black-headed rascal. An imp of mammoth proportions, saved only by his obscure sense of humour!

CHAPTER 17

AN UPSIDE DOWN CHRISTMAS

Plans for Christmas 2009 started to go awry when my lovely daughter-in-law, Jo, went into hospital with severe ulcerative colitis and was threatened with surgery. Martin, Jo, Maggie and Charlie were meant to be spending Christmas with me at Nick's new house in Ireland. Claire had already chased the sunshine and was (busy?) soaking it up on the beaches of Ko Lippe, an island off the coast of Thailand. Jo hoped that a new expensive drug, not prescribed by NICE, would mean that she would be out of hospital for Christmas. I still intended to take William to Nick's, until the snow fell and paralysed most of the country's motorways. Apparently in Ireland, they do not salt roads. They grit main roads, and the snow quickly becomes impacted and turns to ice. Nick left his house and found that he was unable to control his car, so he invited two of his builders to push him back home! Earlier in the day, one of these intrepid guys had kindly brought him a copy of *The Daily Telegraph*, so that Nick would not have to venture outside! When I heard this, I changed William's and my ferry tickets and hotel booking for a week later, when I hoped the snow would be history.

So on the day that had originally been scheduled for my departure, I went to M&S and bought a week of meals to microwave, as my stove had been sold. I bought two bags of coal and battened down the hatches to ride out the icy weather.

Nick telephoned to report that he had been involved in an accident on the sheet ice outside his home, at the exact time that I was previously destined to arrive. One side of his VW Golf was severely dented and the windows were smashed, but fortunately the air-bags exploded into action and saved him from being covered with shards of flying glass. Happily, he was unhurt, but obviously shocked. The next day he telephoned to announce that his water tank was frozen up and that he was without hot water. The following day, he telephoned to say that he felt trapped in his home, but was spending the time watching the foxes and hares becoming increasingly bold as they foraged for food. Two young foxes took to skating across his pond with a series of forward and reverse edges followed by a triple lutz or two, before spiraling off to find a hare to jug for Christmas lunch.

I was invited to Martin's for Christmas Day. Jo was out of hospital, but feeling very weak, so Martin cooked the turkey with all the trimmings. It was a great culinary success and thoroughly enjoyed by the whole family. We had started the day at their local pub, where it was good to meet their neighbours, who had been so kind to Jo while she was in hospital. All the children sat at one table and each of them seemed to be poking the living daylights out of a pink, mini computer screen with a knitting needle. No-one was speaking, but they were communicating via their electronic links.

I left Martin's early for two reasons: firstly, I wanted to be home by dark in case the roads iced over and secondly, I was anxious that William was not left alone for too long. When I arrived home, Wills followed me around with his nostrils glued to my trousers. He could smell Bob, Martin's dog, and was, I guess, rather envious. Or did I smell of turkey? This may have accounted for his Mummy-ish behaviour, where he danced around me with his nose glued to my knee with no daylight in between. That evening, I saw the self-same manoeuvre on the 'Strictly Come Dancing Christmas Competition', when I was delighted to see Ali and Brian win the coveted prize. They were very popular winners, as they had danced exceptionally beautifully as one unit with their romance shining through every sensuous step and each snatched smile. It was a joy to watch their love blossoming on the dance floor.

Christmas came and went without any dramas. Nick spent his time alone in Ireland, sadly without the influx of the Doreys. I then prepared to make my long journey to Ireland with William. A week later than scheduled, we set out. We drove for six hours from Barnstaple to Holyhead, having collected much needed provisions from the M&S service station on the M5.

In North Wales, I stopped at Penmaenmawr, not just for diesel, but more pressingly to give William (and his driver) a much needed stretch after being cooped up in the car for so long. We followed dog-walkers to a little park with a footpath leading to a bridge over a little stream. It was a perfect place for Wills to become acquainted on kissing terms with every Welsh dog in the vicinity. All the dog-walkers chatted amicably and most noted that William was not only the new kid on the block, but by far the largest dog there. He looked supremely handsome with his feathery tail and full-coat, which caught many approving Welsh eyes. We were both delighted to reach the Travelodge, where William stretched out on the blue carpet in pure joie de vivre, his energy spent, as he reached the realms of dog ecstasy. He did not moult as he had done last summer, so I was pleased to be spared the embarrassment of leaving a fawn fur-strewn carpet.

The next morning, we visited Penrhos Coastal Park, where we were buffeted along the beach by the severe prevailing winds, the sort of weather which showed no mercy to man or beast. 'Wind-tunnel-William' loved the experience as he rolled, paddled and skipped his way along the beach. I knew it was important for him to have some exercise before we boarded the ferry, so I let him frolic in the icy gale until my already-chilled fingers, toes and nose had frozen to the bone, with little hope of recovery. On the ferry I left Wills happily in the car before finding my cabin, where I assumed my classical horizontal position in preparation for sailing the stormy seas.

We were one of the first cars to disembark at Dublin Port, as I had paid an extra £10 for a Premier ticket, and I drove through the toll tunnel to reach the M1. It was 5pm and already dark. The rain, which lashed down on the windscreen, was accompanied by bucket-loads of spray from the overtaking lorries. I kept to the inside lane and was relieved to reach Drogheda and find the Boyne Valley Hotel, where Nick was waiting for us on the steps.

William had gone up in the world. The hotel, which normally only took small dogs, had kindly allowed William to stay (a benefit of the recession). William, like his owner, loves luxury. He settled in well on his mat and stayed there happily, while we went to the bar (the restaurant was closed) for dinner. The next morning Nick took Wills out for his early morning call, narrowly preventing him from peeing against the wall of the long corridor.

In the morning light, I followed Nick in his car through many icy lanes until we reached his house. William ran straight to his outdoor kennel, but we had already considered it to be too cold and draughty. He was shown to his new quarters in a large heated lavatory in the garage, where he snuggled down as if he was its rightful owner.

Each day, we took him down the track in Nick's meadow to the Lough, so that he could swim. As the temperature dropped, the lake froze over and Wills decided to walk across to a deserted island. I was panic stricken. I was sure that the ice would crack and that he would be unable to get back. We called to no avail. We yelled: 'Come William!', but were ignored. It was only when we turned our backs on him and headed for home that he ran back to us. For the rest of my holiday, we prevented him from going even to the edge of the lake.

We read in an Irish newspaper that the Garda had strongly advised people to keep off the loughs. Apparently, because the lakes are fed by rivers, the water level drops, sometimes by as much as two feet below the ice, so that there is a real danger of the unsupported ice cracking. A number of icebound pursuits were reported. Someone with an obvious death-wish drove a car onto the frozen lake, carefree kids were riding bicycles, two men pitched a tent and were gaily fishing through a hole in the ice, and there was even some nutter pushing his grandmother in a wheelchair! It may not have been a nice day out for granny! Nick and I made absolutely sure that William was not one of the casualties.

The weather closed in at night to a temperature of 15 degrees below zero. Snow fell. We muffled up snugly (I borrowed Nick's thermals!) and we took Wills out three times a day. Our 'snow baby' was in his element. He shovelled the snow into a long trench with his nose and then ate it! He rolled in the snow, shook it all over us and rolled in the snow again. He was in ice heaven. One day all his Christmases came at once. He saw a fox. Without so much as a hot toddy or tally-ho, he gave chase down the slippery lane towards the lough, gaining ground with every furlong, until he was within a whisper of the fox's tail feathers. Suddenly, the frightened animal sprang sideways up and over the stone field wall, leaving his pursuer with his nose down completely unable to stop. Wills seemed totally perplexed, as he was unaware of the exact location of his prey, who he supposed had evaporated into the thin icy air.

On another similar walk, Wills spied some bulls in the neighbouring field. He stood up on his hind legs, peered at them over the stone wall and barked his heart out. "Aaa Aaa!" I yelled, but he ignored this caution and started to jump over the wall. Fortunately by this time, I had reached my fiendish barker and was able to grab hold of his tail, in time to prevent any un-neighbourly rural incident. I dashed back to the house for his lead, while Nick had great difficulty in holding on to our highly charged dog. Thankfully, we were able to lead him back home without any further incident.

Nick, Wills and I were ice-bound for three weeks. The dog was well stocked with food. For us, the Christmas fare was swiftly diminishing. We gave up reading 'Best before' dates and tucked into whatever we could find in the refrigerator. Wine was (too) plentiful. Our theatre visit was cancelled, as was our dinner date, so we spent our evenings completing crosswords (collected for rainy days), and playing Scrabble. Our Scrabble skills improved exponentially, until we could craftily block each others moves. Life was good (while the food lasted).

One day, when provisions were down to couscous and rice, Nick ventured out to walk down to the corner shop, leaving me reading *From a Clear Blue Sky* written by Earl Mountbatten's grandson Timothy Knatchbull. This well-researched book recounts the ghastly story leading up to the bomb that exploded aboard his grandfather's boat and to the aftermath, when he tragically lost his grandfather, grandmother, friend and his identical twin. I was totally absorbed, as this tragedy happened 25 years ago at Mullaghmore, which the location where Nick had bought a house to convert into a holiday home. No sooner had Nick left home, than he returned. The ice in the road was lethal; there were no footpaths. It was impossible to walk without slipping as the conditions were just too treacherous. We consoled ourselves with champagne coupled with yet another crossword. Our cryptic skills were improving in direct proportion to the loss in the larder.

Miraculously, the road was clear enough for me to travel to Dublin on the day destined for my departure, I cuddled William fondly and asked him to be good. Nick was going to look after him while my kitchen floor was being laid. The minute that I left him, I missed my precious brute. I missed him more than I missed my lover! Nick would telephone every night, so we would keep in touch, but I would have no contact with Wills, just a daily report.

I arrived at the Port a mere four hours before departure, as I particularly wanted to travel in the light. So my journey by ferry, Travelodge and motorway took me further and further away from my beloved pet. I regretted leaving him. I felt I had made the wrong decision.

CHAPTER 18

LIFE WITHOUT WILLIAM

True to his word, Nick telephoned every day. Each day the news was worse than the previous day. William looked for me and was puzzled that I was not there. He raced back from his walk and sat mournfully by the back door. He refused to eat unless Nick was sitting with him. He would eat only if his puppy nuts were laced with tuna oil, when he developed the annoying habit of sucking the juice out of the nuts, then spitting them out! Nick bought him his favourite dried fish treats and some more Markies, in order to tempt him, but the brute was making a statement.

On the second day, he escaped from the garden by squeezing between some newly-planted holly bushes on the front lawn and jumping down the stone wall into the road. He trotted off to visit the little dog at the neighbouring house some way up the lane. I was mortified that William had wandered into the road, as many motorists speed far too fast round the bend. The next day, Houdini made another bid for freedom and I seriously considered coming back to collect him.

Nick hatched a plan. He would walk Wills on the lead every time, unless they were down by the Lough. There were a number of protests to this regime. The objector stood still and refused to move. When Nick pulled him, his collar came clean off over his head. Nick tightened the collar by one hole, which caused Wills to scratch his neck with his hind leg, which was accompanied by a series of death-rattling choking noises, guaranteed to gain a looser collar. Nick released his collar and attached the lead onto his harness. The protester sat or lay down and refused to move during the walk as the whim took him. He was playing up, just like a sulky child.

Life improved for both Wills and Nick when the lake melted around the edges. Once again, my water baby enjoyed his favourite pastime paddling and collecting sticks. All his grumps were forgotten as Nick threw him sticks to retrieve. Most of these were eaten! Wills then decided that he wanted to enter his large summer kennel, so he bounded back from the lake and sat outside the gate ready for playtime in the kennel. Nick was giving this headstrong hound copious cuddles, but still he wanted more. This crafty animal had worked out that if he looked forlorn, he would have unlimited ear fondles, neck nuzzles and tummy rubs.

It was me who needed fondles, nuzzles and tummy rubs. I was missing William more than I could have imagined. The kitchen floor was now eighteen inches below ground level. Each day, a different layer was due to be added. It was to be built up with layers of concrete, insulation, under-floor heating, screed and finally local delabole slate tiles.

I had been living in my guest room, since the staircase to my bedroom was removed when I was out. If I had known, I would have brought a better selection of clothes downstairs! The builders wanted to provide me with a ladder, but I declined their kind and rather perilous offer, choosing to wear the clothes that I already had. At least I had a washing machine in the utility room, so was able to cope. I telephoned Claire to warn her that: "If you arrive from London at night, please do not use the kitchen door, or you will fall into a pit!"

I wore out my microwave and had to purchase another one. I told my builder, dentist, window-cleaner and anyone who would listen, that I was available for dinner any evening. No-one seemed to think that I was starving. I have apologised to my builders for failing to provide tea and coffee facilities, as the kitchen was closed. They had the key, so were letting themselves in and out. I was becoming rather fat (poor diet and no dog-walking) and lazy (poor diet and no dog-walking).

Nick telephoned to relate how much he was enjoying my water-baby. So much so, that I became excessively emotional and wanted Wills back home with me. I missed my best friend. I could not wait for the kitchen to be completed, so we arranged that Nick would bring his nibs over on the night ferry, the next time he was coming to London in about two week's time. We agreed to meet at Westonbirt Arboretum, so that we could give Wills a walk round the massive grounds. Immediately, I felt comforted. My scamp was coming home.

Out of the blue, I received an email from Jan Stone. Jan was the owner of William's brother from the same litter (incredibly also called William). William Stone, who lived in Minehead, was tall and lanky and loved racing around Exmoor and dashing along the beach. He only had two faults: he stole slippers, but never damaged them, and he ate seaweed.

Immediately, I had a word with my friend, Glennis, who bred Wills. How did it come to pass, that I was sold the mischievous puppy? William's other brother, Frankie, was regularly shown and behaved impeccably in the ring, while he collected most of the rosettes on offer. Now I was hearing that Master Stone was well-behaved too. If my William only had two faults. If only……

The telephone rang: "When can I bring the bastard back?" demanded Nick, who seemed, uncharacteristically, at the end of his tether. Wills had been looked after by Nick for thirteen days. Things were so bad that he was prepared to sail over from Dublin to Liverpool on the night crossing, drive for four hours to Bristol, hand over the brute, and drive back to Liverpool on the same day to catch the night ferry. Apparently, Houdini had tried Nick's patience to extreme limits.

The last scenario exhausted him. The ice on the lake was now melting, so William paddled around the thawed parts close to the edge, while Nick threw sticks for him to collect (then eat!). Suddenly his mobile 'phone rang. After the call, Nick looked for Wills. He had gone. A dog, the size of a donkey, had disappeared! He called his name for a good 20 minutes, during which time he saw flashes of fur dashing across the water's edge in and out of the vegetation, occasionally within a few feet, but always out of reach, only to disappear again from view.

"Why does YOUR dog not come when he is called?" Nick lamented. "Why? You ought to train your dog!" Eventually, Nick caught Wills so that he could lead him back home. I could tell he was more than a little miffed.

I could not wait to see my pal. I knew he was far from perfect. I knew he stretched the rules to extremes. But I missed him more than I could say, particularly at weekends, when the builders were not on site. The kitchen was not ready for William, as the under-floor water pipes were exposed. I decided to keep him in the hall, anywhere, so long as he was back with me. I was extremely excited to be seeing him again. I felt like the protector of a truculent immature puppy – a wilful soul, who was incapable of being tamed. One that I loved with enough love to transgress all his misdemeanours. I decided to list his sins:

1   Not coming when called, unless it suited him
2   Chasing foxes (normal instinct)
3   Barking at bulls (still needs to learn not to harass livestock)
4   Mud wrestling (instinct again – possibly not normal)

Then, to restore the balance, I decided to count his virtues:

1   Affectionate
2   Madly handsome
3   Protective
4   Good with people

The kind of dog everyone wants….if only he came when required.

I met Glennis at The Chichester Arms for some much needed 'proper food'. I related one after another of William's mischievous episodes in Ireland, while Glennis roared with laughter. She was a wonderful audience, as she knew my monster only too well. This was why she gave a copy of *Barking Mad in Barnstaple* to new puppy owners AFTER they had purchased their longed-for puppy. She told me that her ten-year-old nephew, Oliver, had so enjoyed the book that his class at a Primary School in Reading were doing a project on William!

 William had made a name for himself by misbehaving. He was not a good role model for young children, but if it meant that they would be introduced to the joys of reading, then it was well worth penning a record of his many devious exploits. It was meant to be written for adults with an outrageous sense of humour, but I guess ten-year-olds grow up mighty quickly these days. It reminded me of the lure of the *Just William* books, which were so popular when I was young.

There is one author who makes a fine living from writing dog stories. Jon Katz is a gifted author, who has just published a new book titled *Saving Izzy*. I had to lecture on pelvic floor exercises for men after prostate surgery in London, so I saved this book for light reading on my journey by rail. I was not disappointed. I complimented myself on getting an earlier train home and quickly became absorbed in Izzy's defiance, so much so that the journey went in a flash.

When I arrived home, in the dark, I turned on the lights. There was a flash of another kind and I was plunged into darkness. There are no street lights in my rural lane. There was not even a shaft of moonlight on that darkest of dark nights. Not even the twinkle of a single star. I missed my protective dog, who would have barked if anyone was in the vicinity. My torch was upstairs by the bed. The stairs were missing! Apparently old people always keep a torch to hand at night, so I was no different! I popped the car headlights back on, but still was unable to illuminate the fuse box. I lit a match, tracked down a scented candle, found the step-ladder and successfully tripped the switch. Light was restored. That evening, I re-learned the value of electricity.

I have kept my cottage very cosy ever since the government was kind enough to give me £250 towards my heating bills. So the day that I was happily meeting Nick and William, I woke early, peered outside and was horrified to see snow about. I drove gingerly along the A361 heading East, with the sun streaming into my eyes, which obscured my view of the icy conditions. I soon collected a queue of cars behind me, until I reached the M5 where, thankfully, the motorway was clear. I met Nick at the Arboretum as planned. Both he and Wills looked shattered. Apparently his car had been on the top deck of the ferry, which was open to the elements, but worse still, the boat rattled and vibrated like a spin-drier all night. Nick had no sleep. From the look of him, William had been awake all night too. To make matters worse, the car would not start after the journey on the ferry. It had to be pushed out of the way of the disembarking lorries and a 'man with a van' had to jump-start it into action.

I did not get the reception from Wills that I expected. He had a woeful, hangdog, expression and seemed unable to smile. On the way home, I popped into John Lewis to look for kitchen cupboard handles and chose a larger one than the kitchen designer had provided. William crashed out in the boot of the car. It was not until I came home, that I realized I had chosen the very same sized knob! The next day, I found the very knob that I wanted at Homebase. It was just the size that I required.

Chapter 19

RE-UNITED (AND AN ACTIVE NIGHT)

Wills perked up like a meerkat as I drove up the lane to my cottage. When I shut the wide wooden gate and let him out of the car, I received the warm, wet, welcome that I had anticipated. He was clingy. He was home. We were re-united.

I think that William had brought the snow back with him. In the space of 20 minutes, there was an inch of snow covering North Devon. William knew exactly what to do. He had been practicing in Ireland for this very moment. He rolled and rolled like a runaway steamroller, with his tail wagging frantically, heralding an orgasmic moment of pure hip-wiggling joy.

Claire arrived from London with Pablo Dos, her fluffy, white, lop-eared pet rabbit, which she kept well away from the rolling champion. The rabbit survived in a cage while we went to the Boathouse at Instow for a belated Christmas dinner with Martin, Jo, Maggie and Charlie. It was a lovely evening catching up with all the various snippets of news. I mentioned that William was very subdued when I saw him, and that I failed to get the rapturous welcome, in the arboretum, that I had anticipated. Martin and Jo commented in unison: "William must have escaped and Nick has bought you a docile, more controllable replacement!". Then they added: "You ought to check his tattoo and chip!"

I took Wills to the vet for his annual kennel cough vaccination and his yearly booster against everything from distemper to housemaid's knee. I did not need to check his chip, as I knew, beyond all shadow of a doubt, that I had the right pet. William had settled back into his normal routine, even though he was now delegated to sleeping in the hall, until the kitchen was finished. However, he was a bit more finicky over his feeding habits, as he was refusing his dried food, unless it was laced in tasty tinned tuna or fresh chicken gravy. Initially, I complied with his requests, before gradually weaning him off this luxury diet. He had, after all, been tempted to eat by Nick, who had provided a range of mouth-watering delicacies to supplement his normal nuts, so it would have been cruel to suddenly stop the trend.

A charming vet, named Tom, examined William's eyes, nose, ears, stomach and balls. The latter test produced an expression of unadulterated ecstasy, not often seen in a male dog of his distinction. It was clear, from the way he rolled on the floor, that he wanted this testicular test to be prolonged into next week. His annual injection went unfelt and unnoticed, but the nasal droplet for kennel cough produced a couple of violent sneezes, spraying vaccine all over the room. Hopefully, he had retained enough of the lively product to guard against all future sneezes, wheezes and lung diseases. This appointment, which Wills had found eminently enjoyable, indeed, far too speedy for his satisfaction, cost £42 for, hopefully, a fever-free year. William was deemed to be in "tip top" condition, so we both left the practice with our heads held high.

William's health may have been 'tip top' but his obedience left much to be desired. Maggie and Charlie came for the night, as I preferred to have them to stay, rather than drive back from their house for half-an-hour in the dark, late at night. When they arrived, William went wild. He loves the children with a passion. He bounced, spun round in circles and wagged his tail right off. I had difficulty keeping him in the hall. The kitchen was out of bounds as it was being updated. The problem would be at night, if the children wanted to visit the bathroom, as William was sleeping between the sitting-room and the bathroom. I decided to sleep on the sitting-room floor. The children had sleeping bags, so they were allocated a sofa each.

After watching 'Skating on Ice' on the television in front of the log fire, we all tucked in for our 'Sleep in'. It was going to be exciting and fun. Maggie and Charlie had explicit instructions to wake me, if they wanted to visit the bathroom, as they had to go through the hall that Wills occupied, and we all knew that William could make them fall down the stone steps with just one wag of his tail. This was the activity that night:

12pm   I took Charlie to the bathroom (a ploy to play with William!).

2am   I took Maggie to the bathroom (same ploy).

2.30am The log fire suddenly burst into flame and lit up the room. I woke in a panic thinking that we were all on fire.

3pm   Maggie woke announcing she felt sick. The only receptacle that I had handy was the fruit bowl. Fortunately her aim was good!

3.30am Charlie fell off the sofa with a thump.

3.40am Charlie woke up and said it was really comfortable on the floor with her head on my pillow (complete with nits brought home from school for half-term!).

4.30am I was kept awake by Charlie grinding her teeth.

5am   I took Charlie, and the remains of her teeth, to the bathroom (to see William?).

6am   I took Maggie to the bathroom (it was becoming a game). After all this practice, I was still struggling to get up from the floor – perhaps more so!

Next morning, it was no surprise, almost a relief, when we awoke early. I bathed Maggie and Charlie and let them get the breakfast while I had my bath. I noticed that their cereal bowls contained a teaspoonful of Alpen and a gallon of milk. Charlie kindly made toast for me and both children made themselves cheese sandwiches. For our morning programme, we had to remember five P's:

Petrol (diesel)

Paper (newspaper)

Park

Parent (they made their mother 40th birthday cards) and

Pub.

I took William and the children to Rock Park in Barnstaple. We walked round the park with Wills, who was delighted to stay close to the little people and then popped him into the car, while I tried feverishly to keep the children alive, as they leapt from one piece of apparatus onto another like an overactive army of orangutans. They visited swings, slides, see-saws, climbing frames, round-a-bouts and even an aerial slide, each apparatus cleverly designed to thrill the children and frighten their grandparents into an early grave. My conversation consisted of a series of squeaky cautions: "Mind your head!"; "Don't trail your leg under the roundabout!"; "Hang on tightly to the aerial pole!"; and "Don't push the swing-bed so high!" I had turned into Joyce Grenfell. I expect my experience as a physiotherapist, when I had seen a plethora of play-related accidents, had made me the bag of nerves, that I had become. The children were impervious to danger (and to my comments) as they flitted excitedly from one piece of equipment to another without a care in the world.

At 12 noon, instead of collecting the children as planned, Martin and Jo were sitting in the Chichester Arms waiting for us. After half-an-hour, they telephoned to find out where we could possibly be! All the while, I couldn't believe how late they were to collect their children. When we arrived at the pub, I reported the nocturnal habits of their dear children, to which Martin replied: "Mum, it is like that every night at home!"

We had a lovely Sunday lunch at the pub for Jo's 40th birthday. She looked beautiful. They had spent a special night out and both looked rested. I felt I had aged ten years – maybe more! It was Valentine's Day, which meant that I had owned William for exactly three years. I decided that he was a doddle compared with two lively children! The roast dinner was a most welcome change from my usual microwaved diet. Even more welcome was my bed that night.

I hibernated until morning, when Dave, the master carpenter, arrived with Oakley, his Jack Russell, to erect my oak staircase. My father would have loved the oak: he would have smelled it, stroked it and examined the exquisite grain. Without doubt, he had passed his love affair with wood down to me.

I purchased a new barrier mat to protect my kitchen floor and placed it in the hall until the kitchen was finished. In the time that it took me to compliment Dave on his expert workmanship, William had destroyed (eaten?) a quarter of my mat! There were swirls of unraveled, curly matting all over the hall. I was not pleased.

At last, I was able to go upstairs again, after a month of being separated from my wardrobe. Importantly, the first item that I retrieved was William's passport in preparation for his anti-rabies injection.

I took William to the vet, where he instantly sprayed against the display cabinet while I was talking to a lady who had brought in a sick cat. I was appalled at his rude and unsociable behaviour. This was not the kind of display that the cabinet was intended for. I was ashamed of my mutt. I apologized profusely and volunteered to mop up the mess. While Helen, the receptionist, was cleaning up, a lovely lady came out of the treatment room with a ten-year-old female Golden Retriever. She wanted to know if my dog was one of Glennis's dogs, sired by Reggie. When I told her that his name was William, she mentioned that she had read both of his books. Fame was spreading locally, even as far as Rosemoor Gardens, where, the previous day, I had seen a few copies of *Barking Mad* in their shop.

Joss, the vet, repeated her colleague's view that William was in "tip top" condition, which was obviously a well-worn veterinary expression, perhaps even a medical term. She gave him his anti-rabies shot (£33.76) and took away his passport to stamp, as she had forgotten to bring her rubber stamp to work with her. I made a note in my diary to pop in on Monday and be re-united with William's precious passport, so that Nick and I could visit France in May.

CHAPTER 20

LOCAL – AND OTHER – WILDLIFE!

Kay, my PhD student from the University of Hertfordshire, came down to stay with me for a week to 'finish' her thesis exploring the best way for women to perform pelvic floor muscle exercises. I gave her the suite at the end of the Barn overlooking the garden and moved the garden table inside for her computer, so she would be able to study without interruptions. Catering would consist of salads, meals out or chez nous - á la microwave. William and I were looking forward to her visit.

My friend had not seen William since he was a mischievous puppy, as for two-and-a-half years she had been totally devoted to caring for her niece, Ellen, who had received a series of treatments for leukaemia at Great Ormond Street Hospital. Ellen was a plucky 13-year-old, who had coped extraordinarily bravely with the severe and debilitating treatment necessary to fight her condition. Her happiest day was when she had hair extensions added to her newly growing tufts of hair to become a beautiful bridesmaid. Ellen had enjoyed *Barking Mad* and was looking forward to reading the sequel.

Kay remembered a bouncy, headstrong puppy, whom we took to puppy training classes together. She couldn't believe here eyes when she saw this massive lump of muscle careering eagerly towards her, with his tail wagging nineteen (even twenty) to the dozen. "He is the size of a pony!" she shrieked.

Although Kay was spending hours on the computer, she always found time to make a fuss over Wills. It reminded me of the time I was writing up my PhD, when I found that playing with my previous Golden Retriever, Mischa, proved to be such great relaxation and comfort. Perhaps I should have dedicated my thesis to her!

Kay spent a week with me and I was sorry to see her go. It was only then that I remembered that I had not collected William's passport! I hurried down to the vet to pick it up lest my memory let me down again.

After Kay had departed, I took William out for his evening walk. He dug his heels in and flatly refused to go. I pulled and pulled thinking that he was being extremely stubborn and willful. The next morning, I knew why. He had been sick in the night. His vomit contained many, many splinters of wood about one inch long. On close inspection, I found that he had eaten a complete corner of an antique mahogany display cabinet. He had turned into a beaver. I took 'chompy' to Springfield Kennels, as I was scheduled to lecture in Ireland. "He has M&S Medical Insurance, if any of these hardwood splinters perforate his gut," I blurted out. I gave Linda my mobile number and, with a heavy heart, I left. I was comforted in the knowledge that Linda and John would take great care of my treasured pet. They had seen him regularly ever since he had been a bouncy puppy. As luck would have it, he suffered no ill effects from his wooden meal.

I flew to Galway to present a Female Continence and Sexual Dysfunction Masterclass and a Male Continence and Erectile Dysfunction Masterclass for Irish physiotherapists, who had travelled from all over Ireland to attend. After two days of lecturing, Nick collected me and kindly took me to Wineport Lodge in Glasson for a couple of days of pampering. I was treated to a wonderfully relaxing aromatic-massage, a manicure and a pedicure followed by a bottle of our favourite pink champagne. On the way down to dinner, I noticed that the eclectic collection of cats on the windowsill had grown exponentially. During our previous visit last year, we had left these cats contentedly coupling, but this year they had sprung apart and seemed too aloof to bother. I respected their wishes, controlled myself, and left them well alone.

The cats may have been celibate, but when I went to collect Wills, he had been anything but! John considered that William, aged three, had become a sex maniac. He had repeatedly mounted a larger (yes, larger) Golden Retriever dog named Basher. Now this fine dog was rather elderly and John feared that his back legs would collapse under Wills's amorous and urgent advances, so 'Casanova' was segregated and exercised separately. Not content with this, my sex kitten rolled up his mat into a ball and performed some Basher-bashing of his own in the privacy (or not) of his pen. John suggested that it may be time for him to have 'the operation', while I shuddered at the thought, until Linda mentioned that there was a bitch on heat in the kennels, who had slipped in undercover despite their rigid rule. Suddenly, all made sense. William's hormones were acting normally for a healthy male dog. I took my rampant animal home and the mat-thrusting abruptly stopped.

At home, Nick was able to view the new kitchen. My new kitchen is white with a black quartz working surface, black ceramic knobs and a similarly coloured AGA, which stands on ancient reclaimed Delabole slates over under-floor heating. It would have graced any house-interior magazine. Nick loved it. I knew he would. I had discussed each stage of the 'build' with him, so he was prepared for the finished result. That evening we went to The Chichester Arms to eat, as he knew that I wanted to keep my AGA spotless!

I was pleased that Nick was able to help me remove my collection of Japanese fans from the totally ruined cabinet in the hall, before lifting it into my car in preparation for its trip to the dump. No-one would want 'brown' furniture in this state and the restoration cost would be more than the cabinet was worth. Fortunately, William had experienced no ill-effects after his mahogany meal, but I could not take any more chances. Antiques and dogs do not mix.

I was preparing my next lecture for the North Wales Continence Group when William started barking anxiously at my five-bar gate. He was warning me that six horses had escaped from the field next door to my property and were galloping merrily down the lane. I alerted my neighbour, Louise, who tried to locate the owner, but she was not at their farmhouse (later I found that she was in hospital). I dialled 999 to alert the police of a potentially dangerous situation for local traffic.

"Heading to the "Ring o' Bells, where? What do they look like?" a young girl from a call centre in India asked.

"Landkey, near Barnstaple, Devon, UK. They look like horses!" I replied. Eventually, the horses were rounded up by the owner's husband and returned unscathed to their field to graze – a possible unpleasant incident happily averted. The police never arrived. Maybe they are still looking for six sturdy stallions somewhere else.

One policeman did arrive a week later. But he was not on the case. He was my nephew, Ian, who had brought his family down to stay for the weekend. He arrived with his lovely wife, Eve, and their adorable children, Emily, Amber and Hugh, who were aged 6, 4 and 21 months. I took them to Crow Point to see the sea and show them the delights of the North Devon coastline. Later, I discovered that Emily was mad on fairies (she even had letters from them and had seen them at the bottom of her garden), so the next day, after collecting Maggie and Charlie, I took them all to the Gnome Reserve and Fairy Meadow near Bradworthy. It was a beautifully sunny weekend, just perfect for flying fairies, as there were no planes overhead because of the volcanic eruptions in Iceland, which had threatened to cause malfunction in aircraft engines across Europe.

Under the silent blue sky, Martin and Jo, with Maggie and Charlie, joined us for the first alfresco lunch of the year in the barn garden. It was glorious. There were ten of us; five adults and five weeny-boppers. Maggie and Emily, her second cousin, were instantly attracted to each other. When it was time for Maggie to leave, she kissed Emily on the lips and poignantly said: "You are my best friend, ever." It was such a shame that my nephew and his lovely family live so far away in Hertfordshire.

I had arranged for William to spend the weekend in the kennels, as I feared that he would be too bouncy for the little ones. I could imagine him jumping up for chicken legs and chasing the little people round the garden or even knocking little Hugh, aged one-and-three-quarters, head over heels. I felt that I would be totally unable to watch William while I was entertaining my family. So Wills was welcomed at the kennels.

This weekend was the first time that I had used my new kitchen. Everyone loved it. Maggie came in and commented: "Gran Gran, it is beautiful." This was swiftly followed by Charlie who said "It is wonderful, Gran Gran." I was delighted as this was praise indeed from my deliciously discerning grand-daughters.

As soon as my little visitors had safely left, I collected Wills from the kennels. The report that I received was good. He had not humped any of his pals, preferring only to bash the living daylights out of his dark green rug. This was not something that occurred at home even with the bitch on heat across the road.

At home, he settled down into his normal celibate routine. Only his ears pricked up when Kay came to stay for another week of 'thesis writing'. William gave Kay intermittent periods of relaxation, when we walked him round the lanes. One sunny day, however, as Kay was holding the lead, I recoiled with horror as I saw a female adder, about three feet long, snaking across the road just in front of us. Immediately, we turned back on our tracks until it disappeared into a field full of sheep. Then, we stamped our feet loudly to frighten her and her extended family, as we continued our walk. Every time I walk down the lane now, I am suspicious that every bent twig lying on the road is a poisonous snake.

After Kay left for Harrow-on-the-Hill, Claire arrived from London accompanied by Pablo, her pet house-rabbit and Catherine, her lovely friend from Brighton. Catherine slept happily in the suite at the end of the barn, Claire slept in the house, Wills slept in the hall, so the rabbit was popped in the conservatory as far away from his nibs as possible. I was not a happy bunny the next morning, when Claire informed me that a disaster had occurred. Pablo had pee-ed over my new cream John Lewis sofa and silk cushions. I swiftly shampoo-ed the sodden sofa and threw the cushions and cushion-covers into the washing machine. While I had spent the last fortnight feverishly protecting my designer kitchen, in one instant, a beautiful fluffy bunny had christened my conservatory!

CHAPTER 21

WILLIAM AT LARGE IN BRITTANY

Two days before Nick and I left for a two-week holiday to Brittany, I flew to Sweden to present two lectures on 'Pelvic floor Exercises for Erectile Dysfunction' at a Conference for Scandinavian physiotherapists. When I say flew, it was more a matter of driving 100 miles to Bristol airport, flying to Amsterdam, changing planes for Copenhagen, then jumping on a train bound for Malmö, a journey that took me further and further away from my holiday packing.

On my return, Nick arrived from Ireland and collected me in his recently-valeted Range Rover. With much difficulty, we hoisted Wills aboard (literally) for the journey to Plymouth, then let him out for a run on the Hoe, before sailing at 10pm. Once aboard, Wills stayed in the car (no kennels on this boat), while Nick and I slept the night in our cabin. Early the next morning, we arrived in Roscoff and drove to a nearby car park for William to uncross his legs, empty his over-extended bladder and have a much needed stretch. Eventually, after much cuddling, cooing and cajoling, he deigned to clamber back into the boot. Nick drove us to Perros Guirec, where we had rented a 'villa-by-the-sea'. This title alluded to a view of the sea solely from the garden when standing 'en pointe' like a ballerina. Thankfully, the garden was enclosed and suitable for William's needs, once Nick had blocked up a dog-sized hole with a garden chair. The garden wall was only three feet high, so we were very aware that our monster could step over it at any time without over-exerting himself one little bit.

The villa was not without some serious flaws. The heating came on only at night, which meant that we were oven-roasted in bed, but chilly in the evening, when it ceased to function. The heating timer was broken. When we turned off the heating, the bathwater ran cold. The towels provided were like miniscule guest towels and, typical of a coffee-drinking nation, there was no kettle.

We had arrived on a Sunday when the shops in France were firmly shut, save for the Boulangerie, which sold scrumptious croissants for breakfast the next day, so, fortuitously, we were forced to eat out on the first evening, leaving Wills in the garage room he had bagged, to sleep off his energetic visit to the pink granite rocks at Ploumanac'h that afternoon. The next day, we drove to the Leclerc supermarket, where Nick proudly produced his Leclerc trolley token, which had been safely squirreled away since our last visit! We stocked up with food, a generous amount of wine, a large turquoise bath towel for me (which came complete with hand-mitts), a travel kettle and a washing-up brush (also for me).

Shops in France seem to spend the majority of their time tightly shut. They close all day on Sunday and Monday and for a maddening hour or two at lunchtime, just when we needed them most. They were also closed for Ascension Day. We became adept at looking at the opening hours on the shop windows and organizing our day accordingly. My favourite leather handbag shop had a closing-down sale which started at 9 am one Wednesday. We rose early to beat the rush and were amused to discover that I was the only one there! I found a belt that matched my new green sandals that Nick had kindly bought me, but I quickly became jaded when it failed to meet around my croissant & wine inflated waistline. The remedy was clear: either cut the croissants and wine consumption or, look for a larger belt. We continued shopping.

We found some new deserted beaches displaying pristine white sand, just waiting for our newly-combed dog to roll in. He was going through 'le grand moult', so he rolled all his loose fur away and replaced it with multiple layers of sand, taking great care to cover every inch of skin by using a selection of intricate moves. He was in canine heaven. We left the beach with more grit on our mutt than was left on the shore. Eventually, the boot of the previously pristine car became 'beach Range Rover'. As the days rolled by, William became braver and ventured further away from us. Unfortunately, with sand-filled ears, he also became deaf to our shouts, so we had a few incidents where he caused great consternation by vanishing from view. I had bought an identity disc from the leather-shop in Barnstaple, carefully engraved by the manager with my 0044 mobile telephone number, but each time William disappeared and I waited anxiously for a call, he came bounding back as if all was well with the world.

One time, my escapologist decided to make a bid for freedom, when trotting from the garden back to the garage. Nick caught up with him on a building site, about fifteen houses away, where he cornered 'the bastard' (Nick's exasperated expression!). After this, we were careful to use the lead when walking him from the garden to the villa and from the villa to the car. Even though he had an ear tattoo, a microchip, and an identity tag, I was frightened that he would run into the road and become the next freshly-squashed casualty. We had a dog who failed to come when we called and was hell-bent on escaping. He had a chip on his shoulder. We had a chip on ours.

One of our favourite places, which we had visited on previous holidays, was Huelgoat, where there are many wonderful walks in the shade of a dense forest. Unfortunately, there was no space to park at the popular entrance by the lake, where mammoth-sized, pink granite boulders were deposited in a bygone age alongside a beautiful babbling brook. We circled the forest and parked at another entrance, keeping young William on the lead until two classes of French children, who were out for a jolly, had passed. When there was no-one in sight, we released Wills to explore the sights, sounds and smells of the undergrowth. The trees were bursting with an array of light-green leaf. Life was perfect.

As if by Walt Disney magic, two young deer came nose to nose with Wills. They looked as if they were about to kiss. It was a touching moment, until our monster gave chase, fur flying, body lengthening, legs thundering at a million miles an hour, maybe more. All three animals disappeared from view in a nanosecond. In shock, we called: "William, come!" repeatedly. We screamed: "Come, William!!" again and again, but there was not even an echo or a rustle of life. I was scared witless in case this deer-chase would cross the road, leaving William maimed or worse. I ran back down the path calling to my crazed, wild animal. He had gone. We had lost him for ever. We yelled and yelled and refused to give up the search.

Eventually, after all too long, I found one exhausted dog cooling off in a mountain stream. He was completely submerged in the icy water hell-bent on lapping it dry. Nick calmly replaced his lead and we continued our walk. The hunter was shot to pieces. Tigger had lost his bounce. For the next two days, he dragged himself around like a hound with attitude, like one who had been out-smarted by a fox displaying superior intelligence. We discussed at length the possible scenarios that could have resulted from this chase: an injured deer or dog; a dead deer or dog. It was unthinkable. We coped by sadly eliminating the lovely forest of Huelgoat, with its spectacular walks, from our radar.

We invited our friends Ann and John to our holiday villa for a walk along the beach and then to a 'soup and salad' lunch. Nick had made scrumptious home-made soup for the occasion and had even purchased a ladle from Leclerc. They brought Alphonse, their delightful Beagle, with them. Alphonse had his own agenda. He disliked beaches, preferring to amble along the cliff path. William quickly followed his new companion, who usually lived life as a loner and was used to circling the French fields in his vicinity on his own.

"This is the dog that you nearly killed," said John playfully. As long as I live, I shall never forget the day that I volunteered to take 'Phonsee for a walk and he was run over by a car. The memory of that day will never leave me. It all happened in slow motion. I saw the dog coming from the strawberry fields opposite. I heard the car speeding towards it. I knew that an accident was about to happen. I was powerless to prevent it. Then, I heard the ghastly thump. To his credit Alphonse has forgiven me and still ranks me as a special friend, worthy of much tail-wagging. After all, I was the one who insisted in halting French that the driver take us back to Ann and John's house. I was the one who comforted Alphonse, while he was bleeding profusely and lifted him into the boot of the racing driver's car. I nuzzled his neck. It was a joy to see him fit and well and enjoying life.

Nick and I were invited back to our friends for lunch. Nick always drives. I prefer not to drive on the other side of the road, so I made myself invaluable by map reading. "At the roundabout, take the second exit, – oh! – if you're going to go round that way, it's the third exit!" I quickly added. We giggled so much that we almost stopped the traffic right there on the 'rond-point'! It has caused ripples of laughter ever since, which come over us in waves.

On arriving at Ann and John's house, we noticed that they

had collected another little dog. Apparently, earlier that day, John had found this grey/white shaggy dog wandering aimlessly in the road, miles from anywhere, so he had brought it home. Ann had reported it missing to the local Mairie.

We walked round the shaded path around Bosméleac lake before lunch, watching all three dogs enjoy their own agenda. Alphonse circled the fields, the 'Newby' followed John, his new master, while Wills jumped in and out of the lake to cool down. My water-baby loved the freedom so much that he refused, absolutely refused, point blank refused, to jump back into the car. What do you do with a defiant, dirty, wet dog? I waited for his heart to change and when it seemed as if it never would, I lifted him into the boot and then, as pay-back, I cleaned myself with his towel.

Newby was reunited with his owners the next morning, when a French couple driving slowly past saw their dog playing in the garden with Alphonse. They had not been to the Mairie and must have thought that their dog had been abducted. Ann told them that she had reported the dog missing, so all ended happily as 'Newby' was popped into the car to join an identical brother. Surprisingly, there was no gratitude for saving this little mite from being squashed on the road, nor for taking him for his daily walk!

My map reading continued apace. More than occasionally, I made a hash of it. In my defence, the map was not up to date and lacked important detail. Also, many of the road numbers had mysteriously changed. Oh! And I think some of the towns had changed places too. To complicate things further, in Northern Brittany every town begins with the prefix 'Tré' or 'Plou'. Towns have similar names. Expertly, I directed Nick to Pontrieux instead of Portrieux some 20 miles away. He was very stoical at the time, but I knew that this teeny-weeny error would leap off his tongue the very next time he had a sympathetic ear. To pass the time and mainly to entertain myself, I gave towns more friendly names, so Guingamp became Ging-gang-gooly-gooly and naturally Pléguien became Penguin. We passed through this latter town and Nick said nothing. He would not give me the satisfaction of recognizing this town, well, not until a good few miles had passed.

The Spring weather continued to improve. The wind dropped and the sun popped its hat on. We were continually concerned that William should have ample walks, copious water and always be parked in the shade with the windows open. This last requirement posed the biggest problem. It reminded me of the time when I ran an old Austin Cambridge, which I had either to crank (impossible) or bump start (possible as I lived on a hill and worked at West Herts Hospital, which was situated on a hill!) and the abject difficulty of finding a petrol station on a hill that gave quadruple Green Shield stamps! My brother, Alan, had sold it to me for £20. After four years, I sold it for £30 to a friend who, sadly, used it as a chicken run. I often wonder what happened to FLY 408? I regret not keeping the number plate.

We spent a good deal of time searching for a restaurant for lunch with a shady car park. Our best find was a delightful restaurant just North of Binic, which was next-door to a supermarket with a covered parking area. One day, we took sandwiches (always chicken for William) onto the beach and sat under the shade of a tree, but our alfresco lunch lost its appeal, reminding me of the trauma of many a childhood picnic, when my sandwich slipped into the sand!

William stopped turning somersaults when sandy chicken sandwiches appeared. His ears pricked up, his dark eyes glistened, and his tail wagged right off as he sat waiting for his lunch, while trying not to lose too much fluid drooling. He can never get enough chicken. He loves crispy dried fish cubes, tuna too, but, at home, barks incessantly if he can smell roast chicken. In France, we found a dried food that became an instant hit. It was rather expensive, but obviously deemed delicious by our discerning dog. It is called Royal Canin (Golden Retriever variety) and must contain all the vital ingredients necessary to make a healthy and lively dog.

We took our exceptionally energetic dog to our favourite beach near Louannec, East of Perros Guirec, and found that there was a large intimidating male dog already occupying the cove. Plan B was called for. We turned left along a cliff path overlooking another breathtakingly beautiful deserted beach. A 'eureka' moment led us to some very steep (and deep) steps with a rough rope handrail, well - just a series of ropes, descending vertically to the seashore. We allowed Wills to shin down first, lest he buckled our knees and sending us hurtling onto the pebbles. With great difficulty, I climbed down the deep steps and made it safely onto the beach. After a lovely walk with much stick throwing (from me) and paddling (by Wills), we turned back on our tracks.

William bounded across the beach and up the gigantic steps like a greyhound on speed. I said to Nick: "This time, he really has gone." We called and called until our voices were hoarse. There was no sign of him. The coastline was quiet apart from the rhythmical lapping of the waves. We had lost our dog. Nick followed as fast as he could, leaving me struggling to cross a line of pebbles. As I wobbled precariously, I was anxious not to make matters worse by twisting or breaking an ankle. Incredibly, Nick found my monster patiently sitting at the top of the steps, wanting to know why it had taken us so long! It was a melting moment, which showed us that he was capable of being sensible, if it suited him. Nick slipped the lead on, and when I had grappled my way up the cliff with a series of novel rope-climbing techniques, which would have been frowned upon by more athletic mountaineers, we took him back to the villa.

When we made our last trip to the Leclerc supermarket, I spent a good deal of time choosing a special bottle of brandy to take home to my neighbour, John, who had kindly volunteered to fill my old Butler's sink with fuschia plants while I was away, in exchange for a bottle of his favourite tipple.

The day before we sailed home, with the help of a series of hand-written reminders, we remembered to take Wills to the vet for his statutory tick and echinococcus treatment. When he was a puppy on his first trip abroad, we had forgotten this essential appointment and, when we eventually remembered exactly what day it was, we had to zoom back from a day out. The lovely vet in Perros Guirec was clearly English, but I struggled to speak to her in French to make her day (and mine) more exciting. As she rammed a tablet deep into his throat, she told me how enthusiastic her dogs were about the glorious beaches of this pink granite coastline. I think that was the drift. She may have said anything. Memo to self – bring a French/English dictionary next time – go to classes – stop being lazy and relying on Nick's fluency in French.

The night before we left, Nick packed the car while I cleaned the property from top to bottom. William had deposited swathes of blonde fur in a number of most unlikely places. We popped our moulting-mongrel in the garage room and moved the furniture, so that I could vacuum every inch of the floor until there was no evidence that a previously furry monster had used the villa to de-fluff.

On our leaving day, we took our intrepid four-legged holiday-maker to his favourite beach for a last energetic run before popping him into the car for the long journey home. We had a smooth daytime sailing from Roscoff to Plymouth and while he was resting in the boot, we enjoyed an afternoon in the privacy of our cabin.

CHAPTER 22

A REQUIEM AND
SEVERAL WELCOMES

Nick stayed the night at home with me before setting off for his long watery trek back to Ireland. In the morning, when I removed his breakfast croissant from the AGA, it was black. Not slightly singed, but black. "That is just how I like it," he said nobly. I offered him my cold croissant, but he insisted that he liked it that way. I felt a failure. He had provided some exquisite meals during the two weeks that we had been together in France and now I couldn't even warm up a croissant in my fantastic new kitchen. If he expected perfection, I was falling short.

I had returned to an over-sized collection of telephone messages, mail and emails, which took two days to clear. I settled back to my life playing tennis, taking William for walks, treating patients, lecturing, supervising students, dabbling with research and having summer visitors. To add excitement to my life, I was seeing Nick again in London in a month's time

I watched TV again. On *Britain's Got Talent* I was enthralled to see Tina perform to music with her rescue dog, Chandi, a grey/white collie/cross. This amazing four-legged trouper kicked her front legs, then her back legs in time to the music, rocked her head from side to side, twisted around backwards, forwards, sideways, every which way in a series of intricate dance moves, before finishing seated on her hind legs cuddling a cane with her front paws. I wondered if it was fair that the human performers, who had spend hours and hours perfecting their acrobatic routines, had to compete against such a talented dog.

I considered asking Tina to train my headstrong mutt, but I do not think, even with her expert tuition, that my pedigree pooch could rise to such an occasion. He clearly does not have the necessary helping of eager-to-please genes. While Chandi was destined for show business and beyond, Wills was hell-bent on heading, at a million miles-an-hour, for the naughty step.

I was scheduled to present two continence and sexual dysfunction study days to physiotherapists and nurses in Berkeley, just North of Bristol, the following weekend. I even had delegates arriving from as far away as the USA and Brazil. Wills was taken to Springfield Kennels, where he hitched up with Basher again. It was not just brotherly love. William followed this elderly Goldie around, sticking to his side with imaginary glue. My young rampant stallion would have loved to have had more, but each time he prepared to mount his pal, John shouted: "No!" until William got the message.

Kay came down for another week of thesis writing. William-Squilliam (Kay's name, when she did not call him Willy-bum-bum) was in paradise. He followed her around and lapped up all the cosseting that was so readily available. The outpouring of affection was entirely mutual and lovely to see. During Kay's visit, I was unable to answer a telephone call in time. I dialed 1471 and rang back and spoke to my friend, Dorothy, who sounded dreadfully distressed. Her darling Daisy (William's girlfriend) had sadly died. Daisy was a dainty, blonde Golden Retriever. She was everything that Wills was not. She was petite, feminine and obedient. A week previously, this lovely dog had experienced her first epileptic fit and had been diagnosed with a brain tumour. Despite medication, this growth spread rapidly as, in less than a week, she was unable to see or hear and bumped repeatedly into furniture, as she had great difficulty walking in a straight line. Dorothy had to make the agonizing decision to have her darling ten-year-old dog put to sleep. She knew that she had no choice, but needed confirmation by the vet, who sadly agreed. She stayed with Daisy during the final injection, until her beloved pet went limp and was at last free from suffering. Then, the enormous sense of loss hit my friend, rendering her empty, bereft and emotionally distraught. She had telephoned me in tears.

I found that I was mourning too. I became misty-eyed and sad, not just for the loss of Daisy, but for the aching, abject agony that Dorothy was experiencing. I had felt similar suffocating sorrow when Mischa was put down, which had tugged at my heart-strings until I was wrecked and just when

I started to recover, the emotion erupted again and tugged even harder. I desperately wished that I could have taken away some of her pain. I loved Daisy. She was special and had brought so much sunshine into Dorothy's life. I felt inadequate. Helpless.

I telephoned Glennis to tell her about Daisy. She was saddened to hear the news and mentioned how often in life the news of a death led to news of a birth. In this case, it led to nine births. Glennis's Golden Retriever, Saffi, had just given birth to a large litter of puppies: two bitches and seven dogs. She could have placed the girls several times over, but she needed homes for the dogs. Her comment: "Everyone must have read your book – no-one wants males!"

The next day, I telephoned Dorothy to see how she was coping. She was more concerned about her 12-year-old grand-daughter, who had howled hysterically when she heard the tragic news. Gemma had known and loved Daisy all her life and felt she could not live without her. I gave Dorothy Glennis's condolences and told her about the kind offer to find a puppy from one of her many contacts in the Golden Retriever world, when, and only when, she was ready. Dorothy wanted a puppy, one that would live longer than ten years, but not yet. Not yet.

I unloaded my sadness onto Nick, who was very sympathetic and understanding. After much discussion about losing precious pets, he eventually added: "A brain tumour, I am very sorry, but at least that is one thing that it is impossible for William to have." I took my empty-headed dog for a walk to ease the pain, while I contemplated the meaning of life.

Later that day, my dizzy dog decided to take himself for a walk. I was struggling to make my virus-ridden computer behave, when I glanced out of my office window and saw that my recently-mended five-bar gate had blown open. I quickly called: "William!" and feverishly searched the garden, but there was no sign of my beloved pet. William had escaped. I picked up the lead and ran down the lane. Half-a-mile away, I saw a blonde tail wagging itself into a frenzy of excitement at the entrance to a field, which was filled to the brim with nursing sheep and suckling lambs. I yelled: "William, come!" and, miraculously, he thundered up the lane to greet me. I gave him the warmest of welcomes, as it was great to be reunited again. How many times can a dog run into the road and be safe? I was amazed and thankful that he had not entered the field – he could easily have shinned under the gate or even stepped over it without too much of a leap.

My gardener volunteered to secure the gate-latch to avoid another break out, and importantly, to prevent the farmer from carrying out his vile threat. This hard-hearted land-owner had said that he would shoot William if he annoyed his tenant's sheep. For three-and-a-half years I have kept Wills away from the sheep. How many more years can I keep him safe from harm?

A week later, William and I were deafened by a series of booming gunshots amplified by the two hills that guard my cottage. I felt as if I had entered a war zone. The cottage shook and the windows rattled close to breaking point. The shooting continued all evening and each time the shot was fired William trembled uncontrollably. I had never seen him shake with fear before, so this was a ghastly new experience. I was totally unable to console him. I tried to comfort him with cuddles, but it made no difference. He spent the whole evening pressed closely to me with his fur vibrating against my legs. He was a quivering wreck.

The next day I asked John if he had been shooting rabbits for dinner and was told that I had heard the farmer taking a pot shot at his rats. Either he was infested with vermin or he was a very poor aim. I felt like borrowing a Jack Russell to complete the job for him. These terriers were specially bred in North Devon (they have even had a pub named after them in Swimbridge). They are excellent ratters and take their chosen profession very seriously and, even more importantly, there is no firearms boom or ricochet, as each dog is as quiet as a mouse.

William was as quiet as a foghorn when Tarka arrived to stay. This delightful black Labrador came for the weekend with my good friends, Jane and Robert. The two dogs bonded immediately and enjoyed visiting Crow Point with us on the first day and Saunton Sands on the second. There was precious little sand at Saunton, as it was high tide and the remaining space was filled with silhouetted black figures. At the car park end, there were surfing competitors in shiny black wetsuits, while further up the beach there was a bevy of black Labradors, each wearing an identical red collar. Tarka was easily identifiable as the one who was shadowing her new blonde boyfriend. They looked good together. Wills puffed out his feathers and towered protectively over his sleek new girlfriend. He had forgotten all about his devotion to Daisy for he now loved another. How fickle. How very William.

On the last day of their visit, both dogs swept in and out of the River Thele, as we walked along the Tarka trail towards Bishops Tawton, to lunch at The Chichester Arms. However, our path was unexpectedly blocked by some bullocks (as it had been when Wills was a puppy), so rather than tempt fate and cause an international incident, we decided to cry 'wolf' and returned home for lunch. Shortly afterwards, Jane and Robert left on their long journey home to Huntingdon. William moped after Tarka disappeared. I was distressed to see my chum so glum. In disbelief, he searched the house and garden in vain for his new pal. He instigated a one-dog-protest by refusing to go out at night and even had to be dragged outside by his toenails the next morning. We had enjoyed every minute of their stay as it had been great fun, even though we had walked our feet off until they were hanging limply by a thread.

While I was reconnecting my feet, Nick surprised me by announcing that he was now ready to give a home to two fully trained adult Flat Coat Retriever dogs. As Chris's bitch had not been mated, I offered to scour the internet and found that there were no fully trained adult Flat Coats for sale from Rescue Centres or from breeders. Not one in the whole of the British Isles. After much searching, I contacted High Hazel Gun Dogs from the Nottinghamshire/Yorkshire border and found that their Flat Coat Retriever bitch had recently given birth to a litter, which luckily included three males. They were just one week old. Suddenly a trip to the wilds of Yorkshire seemed a good idea! Alan was willing to train two of these puppies (at a price) and deliver them to Ireland as the real McCoy. Nick also suggested that William could board and undergo some of the training with them.

My monster certainly needed further training. The previous day, I had entertained my friends, Sally and Jennie for a thoroughly decadent (and delicious) cream tea when Wills had been a pain. Frankly, I was embarrassed. He jumped up at each of my guests when they arrived, despite my intervention, and refused to lie down in the kitchen while we were enjoying our tea. It was a hilarious afternoon, but marred by a cacophony of continuous commands to my over-excitable and deviously defiant dude.

The next day, Nick telephoned to say that he had purchased two one-week-old male Flat Coat Retrievers from Yorkshire. They cost £675 each. He was busily trying to think of names that he and they could live with. We considered Bushey artists, all of the Masters, as many Greek gods as came to mind, names of drinks (I had a cat called Whisky, but every time I called his name, my next-door neighbour would stick his head over the fence and say: "Yes, please.") and even precious stones, such as 'Ebony' and 'Quartz'. I liked the idea of Gaelic names, even Irish Counties, such as 'Cavan' and 'Down'. Nick decided he could live without my help when I suggested 'Down' and 'Dirty', so I waited with baited breath to hear a better choice. Secretly, I would have liked him to own puppies called 'Sooty' and 'Sweep'. After much consideration, he settled on 'Kite' and 'Kestrel' in recognition of his love of birds, while I wondered what mischief they would bring into his calm and unruffled life – not to mention the lives of the birds that he fed.

The next day, I went to see nine as yet un-named Golden Retriever puppies at Glennis's house. They were gorgeous and almost identical, so much so that Glennis had trouble picking out the only two females from the litter. I found it difficult to believe that, three-and-a-half years ago, my 'pony' was this small and this breathtakingly cute. I delivered nine copies of *Barking Mad* to Glennis, as she was giving a copy to each new owner – AFTER they had paid for their puppy! I also met Glennis's eight older dogs, who were very quiet and subdued. Even Frankie, William's brother, was well-behaved. I had definitely been dealt the naughty one.

When my friends Pat and Peter came for lunch, I left my méchant mutt in the boot of the car, where he turned somersaults trying to see the new canine arrivals, Freya and Poppy, who were let out in the garden after their long journey. After lunch, we took the three dogs (two delightful miniature dogs and one pony) along the Tarka trail. True to form, William flexed his muscles and pulled my arm off all the way down the hill until we reached the 'Pooh-stick bridge', where I was delighted to let him roam free. There, he roamed a little too free, as he was sexually attracted to the sweet-smelling Freya and kept standing over his prize with obvious intent to thrust her into next week. Peter performed a grand job repeatedly separating the dogs in an effort to spare Freya's elderly hips.

Pat and I were busy chatting and enjoying the riverside stroll, when, suddenly, Peter called: "Have you seen Poppy?" Poppy had gone missing. We searched the length of the path without success. Eventually Poppy was found deep down inside the quarry. She had refused to walk over the footbridge and disappeared down a steep bank into the stone quarry. When Peter called, she managed to scramble back up, but when he walked back over the bridge, she refused to cross it, preferring to bounce back down into the quarry. It was a miracle to finish the walk with three dogs intact.

Another disappearing act happened at the house that my nephew, Ian and his wife, Eve, had rented in Barnstaple, while they were looking for suitable accommodation to purchase in the area. I popped round with welcoming donuts for their delightful children, Emily, Amber and Hugh, and was given a conducted tour of their new home. I was pleased to find that the house was new, clean and bright and eminently suitable for their needs as a family. Suddenly, Eve remarked: "Hugh has just gone through the cat-flap." While we were talking, my great-nephew, a strapping toddler who was aged just two years, had escaped into the garden through an impossibly small cat-sized door.

The next day I read in *The Daily Telegraph* that a little three-year-old boy had opened the front door of his house in High Hurstwood, Sussex and had taken his Labrador for a walk in the woods. Twenty minutes later, after a frantic search involving a helicopter being scrambled, he was found safe and well by the police, having happily toddled for a mile! It seemed as if everyone was hell bent on escaping.

My friend Kay escaped for a few days from the rigours of running her physiotherapy practice to bring her niece down to Devon for a holiday. Ellen was recovering from leukaemia and was much in need of some West Country air. She adored William and his nibs, in turn, absolutely adored her. Ellen, aged 14, wanted to do girlie things, so we booked 30 fingers in for a manicure and 30 toes in for a pedicure, spent hours choosing a new bedroom for Ellen in Laura Ashley and then impulsively decided to see *Toy Story 3* in 3-D in the local cinema. After seeing this amazingly clever film, I was staggered to find that I was the only one of us who had blubbed their way through the last half-hour! I rushed my hard-hearted friends back home, when I calculated that William had been left for almost six hours. Fortunately, Kay had walked him in the morning, but when we opened the door our guilt evaporated, as we were given a hearty reception that we definitely failed to deserve, with not a tear in sight.

The next day, we took the pony to Crow Point to enjoy a little light swimming and some much-needed partying with other dogs. When he rushed up excitedly to two spaniel puppies, they were led away into the dunes. William gave chase as if his life depended on it. Kay followed in hot pursuit until she fell over, followed by Ellen, who also tripped over her flip flops. William was causing havoc in his wake and was solely responsible for two grazed knees. Kay eventually caught him by the car in a crowded car park. This fiasco had happened because Wills does not come back to me when he is excited. Escaping to be with puppies was infinitely preferable to being with me. I sighed.

Then, I thought about it some more and realized that I was no different. The next day, I was opening my front door (boycotting the cat-flap) and escaping once again to Ireland to see the 'forty shades of green' that make the Emerald Isle such a joy to behold. I was taking William with me, so that he could enjoy Ireland, this time in summer, and hunt for Celtic leprechauns, cluricauns, far darrig, silkies, banshees, and changelings under each green blade of grass.

CHAPTER 23

SUMMER IN IRELAND

A new ferry service was in operation from Swansea to Cork. This meant that William would be in the car for two and a half hours en route to the ferry, where he would spend the night, and then travel a further four hours on his way to Nick's house. This was infinitely better than the long slog up to Holyhead, which had previously taken six hours, or could be more if there was congestion of traffic. Our booking cost a whopping £506, but we did save the cost of a hotel. I decided to see if my Sat Nav would work in Ireland and direct me all the way up the country to Nick's house.

I arrived at Nick's house overlooking Lough Sheelin shattered and exhausted. I had not slept well on the ferry even though the sea was calm. Happily, my Sat Nav worked well in Ireland, but took no notice of the new motorways built with European funding and the many recent changes to their road systems. I had been kindly sent directions by Nick, which I cleverly pinned up to the dashboard – a full proof method – until they fell on the floor out of arms' reach. It was a busy journey listening to the voice of my friendly Sat Nav man, while checking the page of directions and looking for place names and road numbers. William coped well and on arrival we immediately rushed down to the lake so that he could swim. My water baby was now ace at collecting sticks, which we had hurled far into the lake, and clever enough to bring them back to us, before he shook half the lake over each of us in turn causing ribald merriment to the un-drenched victim.

I had meant to write a whole chapter on William's misdemeanours in Ireland, but he behaved impeccably, yes, totally, wonderfully, surprisingly impeccably. He was now three and a half and was maturing into the kind of dog that I had previously only dreamed about. 'Just William', the barking mad inhabitant of Barnstaple, had evolved into a happy, handsome honeybun. I was amazed. He loved his large kennel and after the many walks down to the lake rushed back to the safety and comfort of his luxury holiday home, without even needing his own outside hot and cold shower.

When Margaret and June, our friends from Bushey came to stay, William spied them through the conservatory window and bounced about like an acrobat performing a programme of back-flips at the Olympics, until they came out to join him and awarded him a justly deserved Gold medal, although it was mainly for his handsomeness. He liked to accompany his 'pack' down to the lough, but if any of us were missing, he would look around plaintively for the non-attenders, until they caught up and joined his party. He sat patiently waiting for us to catch up to the white gate opening onto the field and then again at the wooden gate leading to the island and onto the shores of Lough Sheelin. On the way, he always took a detour into one of Nick's newly formed ponds, the one with gradual shelving edges, which we named William's Pond. He would stand in it and look at us, just because he could.

One day, Nick and I visited Mullaghmore to see what progress was being made to his holiday home, though, I think 'progress' was too grand a word, as it was being demolished prior to being reconstructed to a new specification. After meeting the builder, we took William onto the beach, where he ran in and out of the water along the beautiful crescent-shaped, completely unspoiled, sandy shore. Whichever way we looked, the panoramic views were idyllic. This was heaven. We wanted time to stand still, so that we could savour the happiness of that stroll. The sun smiled on us and we melted in its warmth; we were glad to be together, a unit, with a dog that we loved.

This peace was shattered by the roar of a jet-skier traversing the bay. William gave chase along the shore-line, all the while, barking excitedly until he was hoarse. Fortunately, there was no-one in his way, as he moved seamlessly from top gear to turbo in his quest to race the jet-ski to the other side of the beach. Amazingly, he won! There were no prizes for knowing what Wills would like in his Christmas stocking this year; this was infinitely more fun than a greyhound chasing a dummy hare. My grandchildren wanted junior tennis racquets, William wanted a powerful jet-ski!

I left Ireland after two weeks of fun. William had behaved

like an honoured guest and I was proud of him. The only hiccup had been when we prepared to leave to visit Mullaghmore and my little saint had refused to jump into Nick's smart, silver Mercedes. Obviously, William did not recognize style when it was there in front of his nose, but after a little discussion, he decided it was best to jump in. On the return trip, there were no further refusals, as he rather liked the feeling of comfort, space and side-windows that luxury provided.

The trip home was uneventful. Nick kindly led me halfway through Ireland in his silver limousine until he waved my little blue golf onto the motorway. The boat was late in, but, fortunately, there was a car park with trees just waiting to be watered. In the line for the ferry for those important people with a pet on board, I let William out for a stretch and he sat at the dock gates waiting for them to open.

"You have a very handsome Golden Retriever," the man in the car behind mine announced. "I have got four of them at home, so I know about the breed." I agreed and drove my pretty boy onto the deck. On arrival in Swansea, there was a car that needed jump-leads blocking the cars on our deck, so we waited a further twenty minutes to disembark. I stopped at the first patch of grass to let my lad empty his bladder. A man in yellow uniform shouted angrily through the wire fence: "You cannot stop there. The police will fine you." His prettiness, William, was equally indignant, but re-crossed his legs to order and jumped back into the car, until we found a patch of grass outside the port building for him to flood.

My friend, Dorothy came to visit for the weekend. Last time she came she had brought Daisy, so I imagined that William would be sorely disappointed. Not a bit of it. He followed her about like a shadow. He adored her. We took him to Instow beach, where he rolled and rolled under our feet until his fluffy fur coat was covered in sand. He behaved well on the beach and even more amazingly, he behaved later in the day, when my son arrived. Martin kindly came to cut the lawn with his shiny new mower, as Barry, my gardener, was recovering from surgery. After an excitable start, my little pony played well with Maggie and Charlie in the garden. Charlie loved him but I had to prevent her from rolling on the ground with him. Dorothy was amazed how huge he was. He was much larger than my six-year-old granddaughter. "He is nearer the size of my grand-daughter's pony," she exclaimed.

The next day, Dorothy insisted that we took Wills for a long walk, even though it was bucketing down with rain. "Dogs this size need lots of exercise," she said. We went to Crow Point at high tide and found a party of wet-suited enthusiasts receiving sailing tuition and another party, similarly attired, having far more fun. This group formed an orderly queue and took turns riding in a rubber dinghy, which was being pulled by a speed boat. William knew exactly what to do. He had practiced in Mullaghmore for this very moment. He hurtled along the shore line racing the speed boat to the end of the beach, before turning round and zooming back at full pelt. The rain lashed horizontally, but did nothing to deter my speed hog from repeating this exercise a further four times with no reduction of speed.

Then, William had a brainwave. He decided it was his turn to travel in the dinghy, so he swam out to join the happy campers. By this time we were so wet that we could have been wrung out, so in desperation I shouted to one young rubber-clad lad: "Please could you capture my dog for me?" To the amusement of the waiting group, this kind lad held Wills in the water until I could fix his lead. I thanked him and in return, perhaps even in gratitude, my racing hound shook himself all over me. The rain stopped in the evening, which was fairly maddening, as we could have had a comfortable dry walk, but even more nauseating, the car smelt of wet dog for weeks.

Dorothy and Terry had been to visit a litter of Labrador/cross puppies and had chosen the most docile puppy, now named Oscar (the name of my late rather grand white Persian cat). She was insistent that her little black Lab would be not only much smaller than Wills, but infinitely more obedient. I waited eagerly to hear that this was not so.

CHAPTER 24

TWIN FLAT COAT RETRIEVERS

The time had come to visit Kite and Kestrel in Yorkshire. I woke late as William had failed to bark. I rushed downstairs to find the kitchen door open and no sign of his nibs. I panicked, until I remembered that I had left the dear boy at Towsers Kennels the previous day! Nick was sailing across from Ireland and would meet me at Melton Mowbray station, where we would be staying for two nights in luxury at Stapleford Park Hotel. I was taking the train up, as I did not wish to travel back down to Devon on the Motorway on a Friday. I settled down to reading André Agassi's riveting autobiography, letting the train take any strain I could muster, while I learned that André actually hated tennis!

Alan was going to keep these puppies in Yorkshire and train them to a high field standard for the next eleven months, even though they would not be used for shooting. I smiled, when I thought of two puppies just one-year-old rampaging around Nick's garden and field. When Wills was eleven months, he chased seagulls into the distance and resolutely refused to return and, on another occasion, he followed a jogger and his dogs out of sight, causing great consternation for a considerable length of time, until he eventually sped back to us. The pups would find gaps between his holly-hedge that had previously been unknown. They would be up and over Nick's stone field wall, before he could find his whistle. I was going to love hearing (and writing) about their many diverse escapades. My smile hurt.

The puppies were gorgeous, just gorgeous. There was no other word that would capture these shiny black miniature miracles. One, who was larger than the other, seemed rather tentative at first, before slowly coming to explore our feet. His

125

stockiness was possibly linked to a gargantuan appetite – he was obviously the pup who supped the cream. Nick swiftly named him Kite. The smaller, more active one, now named Kestrel by default, was two-thirds of the size of his brother and was unable to stay still. He hung and swung from my new *Per Uno* trousers as if his life depended on it. When I lifted him up he nipped my neck with his razor-sharp teeth. Kestrel was going to be a bold, inquisitive adventurer, a chap who would always be on the go – a proper wriggle-bottom. He could untie shoelaces in a nanosecond and still look cute. I loved him.

With great difficulty, I took photographs of the writhing chaps with the camera on my new iphone. The stills were a bit fuzzy, but the video was more successful and delightfully entertaining. Nick chatted to Alan about his training requirements, gave him a large cheque for their board and then presented him with a copy of both my books about William, to show him how NOT to train K2! As we drove further and further away from the puppies, we felt as if we were deserting them. He was going to see them again in two months' time and I knew that I would re-arrange my life to be able to accompany him.

I rushed home to collect William from Towsers Kennels. He was a giant compared with the puppies. As Sean loaded my carthorse into the car, he could not wait to tell me that one of his dog-walkers had read *Barking Mad*. When he introduced her to the star of the book, she was overly chuffed to be allowed to walk him. After reading about his willful, often obdurate, behaviour, I was surprised that she did not turn tail and run!

Kay came down to continue writing her thesis. William Squilliam followed her everywhere; he adored her. She wanted to 'jump' photos of her fan from my iphone to hers for Ellen to see. Ellen was back in hospital suffering from pressure on her brain, but that did not prevent her from asking Kay if I had received her thank you card. I told her how very much I appreciated it, but, more importantly, I hoped that she would soon be able to wake up in the mornings without her horrid headache.

I discovered that William had developed a haematoma on his left ear, which had gradually grown in size until it was two inches long. I telephoned Glennis, who informed me that he had probably knocked it and that it may grow larger before it settles down, but he could be left with a thick ear. I decided to avoid having a dog with a cauliflower in his ear, so I diligently made an appointment to see the vet. I saw his friend, Joss, who made a big fuss of my wounded soldier and gave him a steroid injection to his rump with a view to aspirating the blood-filled sac in three days time. Wills was unwilling to let her pop an auricular-scope in his ear to check for infection and any number of vegetables, so she used a doggy talent and sniffed it instead. It smelt fine. She did mention that his coat felt greasy and that I ought to shampoo it to avoid hot spot, a condition brought on by mites, which irritate the skin, causing dogs to scratch and create sore areas. William made a dash for the door; he had heard enough. I popped him in the car and went back to make an appointment for three day's time.

Kay and I proceeded to bathe the brute the next morning. It was a two-man job. While Kay held our victim by a lead to his collar, I doused him down with the hose. He has always hated the hosepipe, so he wriggled and contorted himself into some strange positions, before using his testosterone-charged strength to break free. Once I had anchored his lead over the gate post, we were able to soap him with the 'Shampoo for puppies and kittens', that I had used only once in three-and-a-half years. Clearly a 'shampoo and set' was long overdue. We rinsed him (and half the outside of the house) until he was squeaky clean, before toweling him dry. During this procedure, he shook himself violently over both of us (and the house) twice, until it was our turn to squeak. Kay rewarded him by brushing his fur into a Mohican.

We took our newly styled friend for a walk round the block to dry in the sunshine. He was two-shades lighter, much curlier and looked a tad effeminate. When we passed the farmhouse, the two huskies, that howl each evening, threw themselves at the gate and barked ferociously like wolves, viciously baring their savage eye-teeth in anger. Both Kay and I could not hold William, as he crossed the lane and barked for his life. The farmer drove past in his car and stopped, so I asked him: "Please can you help. I cannot hold my dog."

"No," he replied. "I am going into Town. Your dog

shouldn't be over there." Kay and I were on our own. We wrestled Wills away from the gate and with much difficulty led him safely home.

I took my silky-soft diva to see Joss. He cocked his leg against the counter and pee-ed before I could say 'Good Morning'. I was embarrassed. William was relieved. Despite his uncontrolled entrance, Joss kindly said: "That is where all the dogs go." As the receptionist hurried for the mop and bucket, Joss shaved the inside of his ear and applied anaesthetic cream to the bald area. I was advised to take him for a walk for 10 minutes and return him with a numb ear. Then, she inserted a needle and drained 2cc of blood out of his ear, before injecting 1cc of cortisone to aid healing. The result was one flat ear for Wills and a bill of £64.18 for me. Kindness to animals was becoming ear-shatteringly expensive.

Two days later, the offending ear had filled with a little fluid. Being a responsible dog-owner, I telephoned Joss, who indicated that I should leave well alone, unless it refilled as before. If it needed aspirating, it would cost another £21, so I watched it closely and defied it to return. After another two days, my defiance was rewarded in spades: William's left ear had returned to its former state, completely matching his other ear for size, silkiness and flop-ability. To complete his recovery, he just needed to grow some ear-hair over the recently shaved area. For this hairy activity, he was clearly on his own.

CHAPTER 25

A RATHER-TOO-LARGE BIRTHDAY

My seventieth birthday came round all too quickly. I had dreaded it for over a year. I had invited my special girlfriends to celebrate with me and make the somber occasion fun. My mother had sadly died from liver cancer when she was just 70 years of age and I was by no means ready to kick any sort of bucket until I had stretched life to the full. My dear father had lived a wholesome life until he was 90 years of age and I intended to follow his example. He used to dance in the Village Hall with 'young' ladies of 50 years of age, and massaged anyone in the village who had a painful joint or two because his daughter was a physiotherapist, even though I had given him no instruction! He was a keen carpenter, who used his love of wood to help people in need of his skills. Also, he was a productive gardener, who swapped his home-grown vegetables at the village shop for sugar and tea as he had done in the war.

I decided to have an All Girls' Night Out at the Barnstaple Hotel with 11 close friends who had shared the highs and lows of my life (and theirs), and who now emerged unblinking into the sunshine. It was lovely to share my day with Ann, who had travelled from France; Claire, from Great Bardfield, who unfortunately broke down en route and had to hire a car in Bristol; Glennis, who bred William; Jane, who had recently had a knee replacement; Judy, from Chiswell Green; Kate from Australia; Kay, my PhD student; Liz, from Honiton; Lyn, owner of Cassie; Sally, my friend who is a sex therapist, and Mary from Bushey.

We met at 4pm to swim or in the case of the non-swimmers to start pool-side drinking. Champagne corks were popped in my room at 6.30pm and the party began. Dinner was served in a private room, where all the guests moved round after each course, so that they could meet each other. This was followed by everyone staying the night and meeting again for breakfast. At dinner, Judy reduced me to tears by her kindness as she surprised me with a speech:

I'm very happy to be the first on my feet to thank Grace for this very generous Birthday celebration!

We each, of course, will have our own thoughts and memories of Grace's friendship.

For me, as we go back more than 40 years, I can say quite a lot!......but I may not!!

We have shared so many good times and on occasions, some of the less than good times, throughout the years of knowing each other.

From those very early physio. days, when we worked at West Herts Hospital, where she always managed to bag the good-looking male patients with her assertive "This one's for me!!" She even tried that one on, one time, when it was my husband waiting to take me home.

I find it amazing to recall that, albeit for a very short time, I was actually Grace's boss. A first and a last of trying to get Grace to do anything she didn't want to do! (Oh dear, William must have gained his stubborn nature from me!)

Kindly, Grace suggested that I apply for the physio. post at Kodak, when she decided to move on to pursue pastures new, with those grander times at BUPA Hospital Bushey, where she changed the Physiotherapy Department from its 'broom cupboard' status to a fantastic facility incorporating hydrotherapy, gymnasium and much, much more.

I don't think that Grace is necessarily a great follower of fashion…but there was an occasion back in the '70s, that I fancied that she was just a tad jealous of my situation, when I told her that I had decided to divorce my husband. To quote you, Grace: "Well if you can do it…..then I can too!!".

Months of spending Saturday evenings together followed our new found situations: planning, plotting, screaming, crying, but always supporting each other. There were laughter and tears in abundance, as we compared notes from our now mutual legal advisor. She fancied our very expensive solicitor! It must have been mutual as my fees were much more costly!

During that time, Grace and I worked relentlessly on the 'highly confidential', delicate and difficult bits of her affidavit, in the bar of the White Hart pub in Beaconsfield.

Job completed, wrapped and sealed in a plain brown envelope, she cleverly secreted the said parcel of well-thought-out words under the driver's seat of her precious car. She promptly forgot it was there, when, years later, the car was sold! She was covered in embarrassment when it was returned to her.

When it eventually came to D-day for Grace, she marched triumphantly out of the Divorce Court in Watford, as she had just been awarded custody of her famous red Porsche... and then demanded to know, as 'Mi Lud' had been so generous, if she could marry the judge! I remember it well....for my part I got a parking ticket for being the supportive friend!!

Our soon to be exes could not understand how we could do 'it' to them....."Don't leave us!" your ex declared, as he couldn't make gravy. Mine couldn't make custard! Yours was very soon replaced by a tool – a gadget that opened marmalade jars. Grace asserted that she did not need a man now.

I know...and I think that we all know that she has changed her mind somewhat on that score...She has come a very long way since then....In fact, all the way to Devon!

Grace, I thank you for your friendship on so many levels. It is our friends that make the world go around. We wish you many, many years of continued good health and times filled with only joy and happiness and of course, lots and lots more laughter!

I was asked to reply, but could only blub my inadequate thanks to Judy and my special friends for coming and to raise a toast to Dorothy, Jenny and Jennie, my absent friends, who were cruising, having surgery and moving house respectively.

On the day of my big birthday, Nick came down to Devon. He gave me a most luxurious and romantic present – a super King-sized bed. He took Martin, Jo, Maggie, Charlie and myself to the Fullam Chinese Restaurant in Barnstaple for a very special celebration. My grand-daughters presented me with dinner plates, which they had lovingly painted and glazed in a special shop in Bideford - I shall cherish them for ever. It was a very special evening marred only by a bump. While she was trying to tame her chop sticks, Charlie fell off her chair. "I did not mean to do that," she whispered as she jumped back up to master the art of eating Chinese-style.

The next Sunday, I invited Joyce, my sister and Peter, my brother-in-law, Alan, my brother and Rosemary, my sister-in-law, and all of our children and grandchildren and my cousin, Claire, and her husband, Karl, to a family Sunday lunch at Saunton Sands Hotel. Twenty-three of us dined overlooking the glorious sands, before walking down to the water's edge to paddle in the sea. Nick had bought me some new purple Wellington boots to match my dress, so I was obliged to wear them, even though most of the guests threw off their shoes and let the sand tickle their toes. The sun not only shone on the righteous, but out-shone itself to provide a temperature of 23 degrees Centigrade, a record for an October day, so all the little girls took off their pretty pink, party dresses and ran naked into the sea and covered themselves with sand before plunging into the children's pool. They would still be there, if the promise of a chocolate birthday cake had not lured them out of the water.

I had asked for no presents, just home-made cards. My sister had found two photographs of me as a baby, one where my mother and father were bringing me home from Springdene Maternity Home in Whetstone, during a break in The Blitz in their Standard 10 car, which she cleverly incorporated into a birthday card. This Clinic is now a Nursing Home which looks after the elderly, so I could return to my roots and still be welcome.

My brother sketched a gigantic William with a diminutive me looking up helplessly at him as he was saying:

"JUST DON'T THINK THAT NOW
YOU ARE SEVENTY
YOU CAN START TO
BOSS ME ABOUT!".

So attaining three score years and ten was far from painful – it was fun. The celebrations went on all week. I am blessed with some wonderful friends and a close family circle. I am privileged to have such a loving partner as Nick. He reminded me that on New Year's Eve, it would be 25 years since we met. This one is for me.

My life is completed by a mischievous, over-grown puppy, the size of a pony. His name is William. For the last four years, he has enhanced my life by providing constant fun and companionship. I hope that we will have many more happy years together. He was my very best Christmas present, a darling puppy, who arrived on Valentine's Day.

AFTERTHOUGHTS

This is the last book in the trilogy about William. I started keeping a diary as therapy while my puppy was continuously misbehaving, as I felt that I had to unload my frustration onto anyone who would listen. Now, aged four years, my large lad has settled down to be a loving companion, the sort I would have liked to have owned from day one. We have come a long way together and during that journey, we have learned about each other's likes and dislikes, failings and foibles, until we have bonded together to form a perfect partnership (unless there is any livestock within sight). You have just read the enduring, and at times totally exasperating, love story of Gran Gran and William, a puppy the size of a pony.

THE LAST WORD

Just when I had thought that William had become a paragon of virtue, Claire arrived from London and he went ballistic. He turned many circles of delight in the new kitchen before lying on his back and with a wicked glint in his eye he spurted four jets of urine up to the ceiling. So weird. So William.

WILLIAM'S PEDIGREE

WILLIAM	PARENTS	GRANDPARENTS
Seruilia Snowball	SIRE Gatchells Lone Ranger	SIRE **Show Champion** Marjamez Midnight Cowboy At Westervane
		DAM **SW Show Champion** Dewmist Serenella (Imp Swe)
	DAM Bedeslea Blushing Bride Via Seruilia	SIRE Seruilia Steamroller Stan
		DAM Bedeslea Black Eyed Susan

BY THE SAME AUTHOR

Barking Mad in Barnstaple The diary of a Professor who was given a fluffy Golden Retriever puppy by her nearest and dearest for Christmas and the total mayhem that it caused.

William: Still Barking Humorous account of the second year in the life of 'the hound from hell'.

Clench it or Drench it! Self-help book for women with urinary leakage

Love Your Gusset: Making friends with your pelvic floor Cartoon book for women with incontinence, sexual dysfunction and an outrageous sense of humour

Make it or Fake it! Self-help book for women with sexual dysfunction

Prevent it! Guide for men and women with leakage from the back passage

Use it or Lose it! Self-help book for men with urinary leakage and erectile dysfunction

Living and Loving After Prostate Surgery Self-help book for men with incontinence and erectile dysfunction after prostate surgery

Stronger and Longer! Guide on improving erections with pelvic floor exercises

Pump Up Your Penis: Easy exercises to strengthen your erection Cartoon book for men with erectile dysfunction and a wild sense of humour.

Pelvic Dysfunction in Men: Diagnosis and Treatment of Male Incontinence and Erectile Dysfunction Textbook

Pelvic floor exercises for erectile dysfunction Textbook

All books are available from
www.yourpelvic floor.co.uk

AUTHOR

Grace Dorey is a Consultant Physiotherapist at Nuffield Hospital, Taunton and Queens Medical Centre, Barnstaple. She is Emeritus Professor of Physiotherapy (Urology) at the University of the West of England, Bristol, UK.